The Unity of the Species

~ Realising Our Potential ~

With Ney ards

Brian Cowa

1 elbor Beog

Chennel Rd

Rish

The Unity of the Species

~ Realising Our Potential ~

Brian Corvin

First published in Ireland, in 2023, under the imprint of
The Manuscript Publisher

ISBN: 978-1-911442-48-6

A CIP catalogue record for this book is available from
the National Library

Typesetting, page design, layout by DocumentsandManuscripts.com

Cover design by Andre Corvin

Published, printed and bound in Ireland

Acknowledgements

I would like to offer many thanks to the eight billion of you out there, who in one way or another inspired, encouraged and helped me to put this workbook together, with a special nod to Rory, Brenda, Andre, and my publisher, Oscar, who assisted me in bringing the work over the line. I sincerely hope that I will get a chance to use it with you in the near future, as we move on towards the Unity, and work to realise our potential.

Introduction

We have experienced a number of very worrying and extremely damaging crises in this century, so far. The first was an economic crisis, which came unexpectedly in 2008. This started in the US, when a number of the larger banks were hit by severe financial difficulties, and some even went under. The trouble spread across the States and then moved around the world. The financial systems of some of the smaller countries almost collapsed before this crisis was brought under control.

In many of these countries, ordinary people had to bale out the banks with higher taxes and austerity controls.

The next crisis affected the global health system. It came out of China in 2019, with very little warning. A virus came into Europe, bought in by Italian holidaymakers and then moved on to the United States, where it infected millions. Within a year, it had spread worldwide.

This pandemic was known as Covid-19 and in little over two years, it had killed off several million of us, worldwide. This was the most dangerous infectious disease in a hundred years, since we had the Spanish Flu, just after the First World War. However, in Covid-19's second full year, scientists managed to produce several successful vaccines, which brought the virus down to manageable proportions, but it lingered on for several years.

Shortly after Covid-19 was brought down to epidemic status, a serious war broke out in Europe. It was a regional conflict but it had global dimensions. The Russian President, Vladimir Putin tried to turn one of his neighbouring states, Ukraine into a satellite state by rewriting history and upsetting the western-dominated 'International Order'. Putin made some veiled threats about using nuclear weapons if the West intervened in the conflict. The dispute remained at a regional level and the threat receded.

What these crises showed was the need for a global authority with real power, which could get the nation states to work together and keep the peace.

There is another crisis predicted for the 2030s. This is Climate Change, a weather crisis that threatens to dwarf the other problems we have had to face. This crisis could cause widespread damage to the world's ecosystems and communities all over the globe on a colossal scale.

The earlier crises came on us with practically no warning, but we have certainly been alerted to this one. We have had persistent warnings from scientists and journalists for the past thirty years. Unfortunately, some countries are only beginning to take notice and realise that we need to take this very seriously. Our only hope is that we will be able to take sufficient action in the short time that we have left before the bad times come rolling in on us. However, it is fairly obvious to even the most ignorant, that no single state will be able to cope or deal with this crisis alone. Whether we like it or not, some global action or shared response is required to deal with what one columnist has described as perma-crisis.

The World Health Organisation and environmental groups like The Green Party have advocated helpful action and made sensible suggestions, but we need greater cooperation with resources, knowledge and enthusiasm, working together in a more focussed and structured way, if we are to tackle and overcome the series of difficulties that have come at us like the plagues of Egypt.

If we are frank and honest, we will have to admit that few of us have any idea of what will come after Climate Change, if we can possibly manage to survive that. It is very possible that there are even more horrifying scenarios on the way. I am writing here about problems and difficulties like mass migrations, gender, race, nationalism, artificial intelligence, world wars, a global power grab or even another virus. You can take your pick. I have taken mine.

No doubt we can just opt out, to muddle through, taking each crisis as it comes. Or we can, through the workbook, start by looking at how we see the past, with a broad, historical perspective and at the changes we have made as we developed and evolved. Then we can look at the present with its current crop of conflicting ideologies, which we need to address before we move into the future. Here, I speculate on what will happen as we move towards the 'Unity of the Species', which I believe is the next evolutionary step that we will take.

In the second section, I would like to look at the effects that change and evolution will have on the individual. In this section, I deal with the different levels of our society, from the individual to the global society, and the changes that we will need to make as we move towards the Unity.

In the third section, I would like to consider evolution and the evolutionists. I want to discuss what I mean by evolution, what we mean by it, what it can do, how it can help us, and how I consider we can use it. Then I want to look at the pioneers of change, who I call the evolutionists. From Charles Darwin, the father of evolutionary studies, to Tim Berners-Lee, the computer scientist who has opened a whole, new way of communication to us.

In the fourth section, I would like to glimpse at the different aspects of the foreseeable future, as I see them unfolding.

Then, in the final section, I want to write a little about 'The Next Step' that we are in the process of taking on our journey to discover the Unity of the Species.

I believe that we are all on this evolutionary journey together, whether we like it or not. In a general sense, we are all evolutionists, and we can all contribute to the process in our own way. I do not consider this as a book of predictions but as a workbook, and I hope that you will be able to use it as one.

Contents

Section One

~ The Three Ages ~

Chapter One

The Past

Let us start at the beginning, or as far back as we can go. To be perfectly honest, we seem to know relatively little about our origins, about where we came from, how we came to be living together on this small planet, or what are the controlling forces that govern our lives and destinies.

I was brought up to believe that God made the world and all that is in it. I did not find this a particularly satisfying answer. Nobody could tell me much about God or what he had been doing before we came along. Although all powerful, he had two failed experiments. First, there were the angels, and then we came along. If He was all wise and all knowing, how did this happen?

When I was a little older, I discovered that there was a different approach. Scientists had an alternative explanation. They seemed to believe that the universe came into existence as the result of a huge explosion, which started our universe 13.8 billion years ago. This explosion is affectionately known as 'The Big Bang'. It seems that all the material in the universe came from this explosion. Where it came from and what caused the explosion have not been explained.

The scientists have less to say about the origins of life on this planet, or our species than the religious, but they claim that the process or project was brought about by the forces or power of nature. I have no idea if nature is a self-starting, proactive and self-propelling force, or if it is being guided and directed in some way or another. Is it possible that the religious and the scientific explanations are complimentary? Perhaps God made the world and nature keeps it going? Or is it possible that there is another explanation, which we have not heard of as yet?

Moving on to look at the human species, it seems that we know very little about early man. The first evidence of human existence seems to have come from East Africa, about two-and-a-half million years ago. Some stone tools dating from that period have been found in that area, but we may find earlier evidence from another area. We think that Homo Sapiens emigrated from this area half a million years later, and these early explorers found their way to Asia, North America and Australia. A number of the human species, including the Neanderthals, settled in Europe but seventy thousand years ago, only Homo Sapiens remained in the area.

At that time, there were bands of roving hunter-gatherers, slowly shifting around the European continent. They depended on plants and berries, fish and small animals for food. Our ancestors continued to wander round the continent, seldom remaining in the same place for very long, until they begin to settle, in an evolutionary move, which is regarded as the agricultural revolution.

This settled way of life was a good deal easier and more stable, with the domestication of animals and plants. Slowly and gradually, small settlements developed, and these grew into villages and towns. These settled communities appointed tribal chiefs and these, in time, raised armed bands and armies for their own protection, and to raid their neighbours' territories. They used flags and anthems to help map out their homelands.

Over a considerable period of time these towns grew into cities with walls, fortifications and castles. Religion came to play an important part in the lives of the people living in these settlements. It offered inspiration and consolation, help and guidance when it came to dealing with the unseen forces surrounding them.

Today, religion is often disparaged and regarded as a negative force, with a regressive influence, but it had much to offer: an optimistic vision, a reason for living and a moral compass in a chaotic world. It has also been one of the great game changers in human history, along with economics and politics. During the Middle Ages, religion played a considerable part in bolstering the social fabric of different communities, helping to keep even large groups stable and was used as a pacifying force and civilising influence by ruling elites.

Religion had a good innings but its influence was weakened and diminished by the Scientific Revolution, which came on the scene just over five hundred years ago. It dates from 1543 when Nicolaus Copernicus's *On the Revolution of the Celestial Spheres* was published posthumously. This asked a number of questions about the Earth being the centre of the universe, and it helped to give us an important new framework for understanding the world that we live in. The new methodology advocates that we should make predictions and follow them up by looking for evidence and proof to back up our findings and claims. It brought us the discovery of new medicines, different ways of doing things and the invention of new machines. This resulted in a huge investment in scientific research of all kinds. The discoveries of Galileo, Newton, Faraday and others followed, and they changed our world mainly for the better. We found a fresh belief in our own abilities and potential.

In the 19th century, the discovery of new methods of mass production of goods in factories and the new methods of transport, led to the rise of capitalism. In this revolution we saw a huge drift away from the countryside and agriculture. We saw huge numbers of people gravitating to large towns and cities. During the 19th century, so much seemed to change. First came steam engines and ships, then electric traction, telephone, photography and the moving picture.

At the beginning of the 20th century, there was a wonderful feeling of optimism and hope. Some people believed that everything possible had been invented. Now it seemed that wars would soon be outmoded and outdated. It was felt that we would be able to travel round the world without a passport, that we would be voting for a world parliament.

The new medium of the movies began to make films about trips to the moon and wars of the worlds, while World Fairs demonstrated the wonders of the new century that was opening before us.

This optimism was cruelly shattered by the absurd madness of the First World War, which was optimistically billed as 'The War to end all Wars'. However, it was not enough for us, and it was followed by an even more ferocious conflict just twenty years later. As if this was not enough, we had a stalemated conflict, which we call 'The Cold War', with nuclear weapons hovering in the background. This fizzled on and off for four decades, and only came to an end when the Millennium beckoned.

Towards the end of the century, we saw the arrival of another evolutionary revolution, blossoming. This was when computers came into their own and began to show a new and exciting way of communicating. Here, we had the promise of a new language, and a surprising new way of bringing us closer together, though many of us are still apprehensive of AI (Artificial Intelligence).

So, what are the lessons that we have learned from the revolutions that have happened so far?

As hunter-gatherers, we moved out from our East Africa homeland to explore the wide world. We managed to survive in many different climatic conditions and we saw Homo Sapiens become the dominant strain.

Moving into the agricultural phase, we saw a change of lifestyle, as we became a domestic species and began to work together in larger and larger clusters.

In the Religious Revolution that followed, we developed spiritual qualities like love and empathy and discovered the nation state. It helped us to realise our inner potential as individuals and communities.

After this, we had the Scientific Revolution, in which we discovered new ways of doing things, through investigation, testing and proving. Most importantly, we discovered that we could depend on our own capabilities to make progress and move forward.

We moved on from this to the Industrial Revolution. We moved away from the agricultural way of life and began to interact with machines in a serious way. We discovered how to mass-produce goods, learned new business methods, and allowed economic growth to become one of our central goals in a new, urban way of life.

Now we have moved into a technological or 'knowledge-based' revolution. We are learning a new way of communicating and we are relying more and more on the machine, in a way that would have seemed unimaginable seventy years ago.

The time between the evolutionary revolution is growing shorter and shorter as we become more consciously aware of what is happening. The next evolutionary move is the really big one, 'The Unity Revolution'. When it comes, we will learn a new way of thinking, working and living together. Of course, we may try to delay it, repeating the mistakes we made in the last century. Hopefully, we can learn from what they did and did not do.

When we look back, we should take note, make sure that we do not make the same mistakes again, allow evolution to guide us, and use it intelligently to discover that we really are all in this together.

Chapter Two

The Present

As far as I remember, a great number of people were expectant and optimistic as the Millennium approached. The American philosopher, Francis Fukuyama wrote an influential bestseller called *The End of History and the Last Man,* which suggested that we had come to an end of narrative history and that are going to experience a peaceful, democratic future worldwide. However, I do not think that we are going to see an end of narrative history anywhere just yet. I feel that we are about to enter a new phase, and possibly settling down to write a fresh chapter in the story of Homo Evolvus.

Before we move too far on, there is a good deal of influential business that we need to clear up before we even consider a new agenda. It is necessary to deal with the problems and difficulties that we face today, because we do not want to repeat the mistakes that we made in the last century. If we do, we will delay the changes that we need to make. We would not be able to stop changes coming, but we could delay matters. In the last century, we lost so much time bickering and fighting, repeating our mistakes, not learning the lessons that could take us forward through the portals of the New World Order, into the brave new world beyond.

Strangely enough, evolution can help us to make the necessary changes, if we use it properly. If we use it in the right way, it will make life easier for us and help us to realise our potential. We need to use the scientific method, as Darwin did: namely speculating, experimenting, testing and using the results. We can deal with the many problems that we face, but we must work together in a new way.

In this chapter, I want to look at some of the problems and difficulties we face and make some suggestions that may help us to tackle them. Some of the suggestions I will make may seem very obvious, while others will definitely sound odd, but we should leave aside our prejudices and see how they work out.

In this century, we appear to have moved into a knowledge-based world, where information, digital knowledge and communications are often more highly regarded and valuable than experience, money and material goods. It seems to have offered greater flexibility to many, and many people are working at home rather than crowding into business offices; though, one wonders if this is bringing us closer together or drawing us apart.

At present we are just beginning to communicate with computers and their offspring, in social media, doing this in new and different ways. We are still at the kindergarten stage and do not seem to have any real idea about how this is going to work out. On a popular level, we seem to be dumbing down with the material that we have at hand, offering reams of false news, scamming the unready, and in a peculiar way, trying to reinvent the wheel, especially on the internet with Facebook and Twitter. At times, YouTube tries to move forward with intriguing talks and, by showing us how to do different things in simple ways.

I must say that I was impressed by the way two American presidents, Obama and Trump, used social media to garner support and funds when they were campaigning. However, in the background there is the fear of the AI 'singularity'. This will come when the digital media meets, matches and even beats human intelligence at its own game. This was suggested by Stanley Kubrick in his movie classic, *2001: A Space Odyssey*, when a computer tries to take over a spaceship. Nevertheless, before that problem comes along to bother us, we will need to watch and be wary of the fabulously wealthy media moguls, who are becoming an increasingly powerful economic force and may soon be in a position where they can control or manipulate politicians and businessmen of all stripes. In this area we hear stories of foreign governments hacking and manipulating results in US elections, and even in Britain.

Hopefully, our children will have a greater awareness and be more clearsighted than we have been, and will be more willing to question politicians, teachers, philosophers, call them to account and ensure that they change things that need to be changed. It is not simply good enough to believe that those in charge know best, or that they have all the right answers. I really feel that we need to find better and more satisfying answers to the questions we need answered today. For instance, will we make the same mistakes in this century that we made in the last? Will we do things in a better or a different way than our parents? Will we go back to the 'old normal' when new crises recede? Will we realise that we need to adapt to new methods and ways of acting when the old problems, like pandemics, wars and economic difficulties pop up again? Will we begin to accept that old organisations, like the UN need to be replaced by new ones, like a Global Federation, which will be more proactive and capable of helping us deal with the further crises that face us?

If we look back at what has happened in the past century, it is reasonable to ask if we would prefer to see things remain the same, with the rich growing richer, the poor growing poorer and the ones in the middle picking up the pieces when our crises recede? It is a shame that we have to wait for an emergency before we join forces and take action in a significant way. It was good to see the World Health Organisation take action during the Covid-19 pandemic, and the scientists come up with several vaccines within a year of the virus's appearance. There have been a considerable number of governments attending conferences to deal with Climate Change, as well as the West's response to the attempted power grab by Russia in Ukraine, but we need to ask is this enough? Can we do more, and in what way?

Unfortunately, it seems at times that we do not want to come together. In recent times, we have had a number of national populist leaders, like Trump in the US, who wanted to 'Make America Great Again', Johnson in Britain, who wanted 'Britannia to rule the waves', Putin in Russia, who wanted to make 'Russia First Again' by launching a power grab in Ukraine. While in the east, Modi wanted to see a Hindi India. The Taliban wanted women to return to a form of serfdom and we find fundamentalist Muslims want a return of the Caliphate. This suggests that many of us do not realise that nationalism is in its dying phase and that change is coming, whether we like it or not.

Nationalism has served us well over a considerable period, but it has become an increasingly dysfunctional project, not quite able to cope with our needs in this century. So, what is the alternative to nationalism, which will meet our needs in our multicultural age?

I would like to suggest globalism, though the process is going through a rough period at present. We should perhaps label the current phrase for the project as 'Economic Globalism'. This vision is perhaps too narrow, limited and restricted in its scope, and it gives the impression that globalism is simply an economic tool.

We need a much wider concept, which could be labelled or called 'Cultural Globalism'. This will embrace sports, arts, food, clothing, education, religion, politics and whatever else we need in our new, globalised world, as well as economics. The Eurovision Song Contest, the Olympics, the Cannes and Venice film festivals, the World Cup and Parliament of the World's Religions are encouraging signs that these needs will be met.

There are other areas, like science and trade, which will benefit from World Fairs, displays and competitions of all kinds, and will be used to bring people together.

There is another area that I would like to look at: the question of the needs and rights of the individual and the communities at different levels. It is important to meet the needs and rights of every single individual. These will be protected in a globalised world by an Ombudsman's Department, which will have offices in every town and city, while the needs of communities, countries, regions will be referred to a Universal House of Justice.

Now I would like to move on to another related topic. This has to do with joining up the dots. If we do this, we can often see the big picture. Too often, we focus on our own needs and interests, so that we only see part of the picture or problem. We often try to solve our own difficulties without realising that there are other factors that are outside our control, or how they may affect others. Sometimes, it is better to talk matters over with others, who may know more or have the means of dealing with a situation. This is a problem that can affect individuals, or even countries and communities. I think that something like this happened before the nations blundered into the First World War, or how Britain tried to deal with Germany before the Second. The British thought that they could deal with the situation themselves and made a bad misjudgement.

More recently, in Afghanistan and Ukraine, there were serious misjudgements, and it is obvious that a world authority or even a Global Federation with real power, would not have made the mistakes that were made. It is becoming increasingly clear that we need a world authority to deal with these situations.

Now I would like to discuss money, finance and the economic situation. The trouble here is that money is being used to judge and value everything today. As somebody said to me recently, we are seeing that money has become the new religious currency. We should not be too surprised when a price is put on our lives and every aspect of them. We can consider this as unbelievable or even unthinkable, but I have read about elderly patients in hospitals left to starve because they could not feed themselves. Or consider our attitude to the homeless, who have been forced to sleep in shop doorways or pitch their tents in parks and canal banks. This suggests a disregard we have in the First World for those on the verge of civilised society, while we catch glimpses of huge migrant camps, where a large number seem to be living in absolutely dreadful conditions, in even the most developed countries and societies.

The air we breathe is still free, most of the time, but it will probably go the way that water has gone. In our area, a bottle of water costs almost as much as a litre of milk, and I would not be surprised if it will cost as much as a litre of wine before too long. No doubt, a visit to the public park, taking mountain rambles, borrowing books and discs in libraries, and visiting art galleries will eventually find their ways on to the money trail. Even going to church or cycling on the open road will be used by different groups as ways to make money.

Jacque Fresco looked forward to the time when cash will be completely eliminated and 'need not greed' becomes the new ethic. We seem to be moving into a credit and debit card system. Though a new system using cryptocurrency has been tried, I cannot see the old currencies being phased out just yet. However, we will undoubtedly move to a global currency before the end of the century.

Next, we come to the question of migration, free movement from one country to another and the displacement from one's homeland. This was undoubtedly causing a good deal of trouble after Climate Change and The Last Great War but after the Global Federation comes into operation and the Resource

Archive is set up, one of the first tasks will be to make 'open travel' a reality.

Finally, I would like to consider the problem of prejudice, of one form or another, usually with regard to stereotypes of gender, race, class, religion or nationality. We usually inherit the negative views from our parents and communities and pass them on to our children. These views, beliefs and misconceptions frequently break down when we get to know people personally and should be part of lifestyle classes at all schools.

When you think about it, these and other problems will need to be addressed in the foreseeable future. I believe that we will need to find satisfactory answers to most of them before we move onto the next chapter of our story. No doubt a number of them will still be troubling us when the Unity of the Species comes into operation, but we will need to deal with them before we take on a new agenda, when we will face a whole new set of problems. We will do it with one important difference, however. We will be doing it together and believe me, that will make things so much better.

Chapter Three

The Future

So, what will we see in the foreseeable future, between now and the end of the century, which will bring us to the Unity of the Species?

I am afraid that our prospects do not look too promising in the coming decades. We know, with some certainty, that a Climate Change crisis is on the way, and that it will be with us in full force within the next ten years. We have had some signs and signals of its approach already. There has been an increasing number of fires, floods, tsunamis, rising temperatures, tides, tornados, deserts and melting Arctic ice. Our governments seem to be waking up to the dangers facing us all. Some have been taking precautions and a number have been working to be ready by bringing carbon emissions down to zero. Despite this, we certainly do not seem to be doing enough as a global community to protect the world from the coming force of the disaster.

No doubt we will weather the devastation from the poles to the equator and live to fight the next crisis. It is difficult to say what that will be but putting on my evolutionist's hat and using the scientific method of speculation, experimentation, testing, with a little imagination thrown in, I would like to make a few suggestions of what will happen. I think that as a result of Climate Change, we will see a migrational surge from endangered and affected areas and lands. We will find millions of refugees flooding into protected and safer areas, possibly from Africa and the Middle East. The great surge movements will cause havoc, strain our resources and cause violent clashes.

Raw prejudice and resentment will come to the surface, in ways we have not seen for generations.

This crisis will probably feed into the next one, which will probably be the most horrifying of the series. In this case, we will probably fight the Last Great War, which some will describe as the Third World War. I hate to think of the horrors it will inflict on the countless millions and the widespread devastation that it will cause around the world. We saw so much of this before, in the twentieth century, that it is extremely difficult to understand why it will have to happen again.

We have often been slow learners in some regards but this could, at least, jolt us into the need to take radical action, and worry about the changes that are necessary when the war finishes. This is one of the few good things that that hopefully will come from this dreadful business. If we can bring an end to wars, battles and conflicts, so that they disappear from the human agenda, then it will become one of the crowning achievements of the twentieth century.

After the war, we will see the setting up of the Global Federation and the realisation that nationalism and the leaders of governments regarded as 'national populists' will no longer be regarded as prime movers in world affairs. These considerations will be seen as a valuable contribution to the Unity project. Unity will be the prime aim and goal of a small number of democratic states, who will plan and set up the Global Federation in the decade after the Last Great War. This goal will be helped and aided by the appearance of a new, global religion. It will come with a growing awareness that religion can play a part and make a contribution to our structural and material development. It will be found that the new religion, Bahá'í will have much to offer: a world-embracing vision, a vast manpower, global networking celebrities, plans for the introduction of a universal auxiliary language, a universal educational system and social programme.

In a world slowly recovering its balance after the Last Great War, people will have begun to join up the dots. This will lead to the setting up the Global Federation, to deal with the rolling succession of global crises. Religion will offer the vision, with the world government as a directing authority. While the Federation will manage to replace the outworn and the dysfunctional United Nations, which had just about managed to cope with the problems of the twentieth century but was completely out of its depths with the crises of the twenty-first.

The feelings and attitude of the people after the Last Great War will develop in very different ways from that of those who lived before. There will be an awareness that we must not let it happen again, which will be widely described as 'Survivors' Credo', and very few will want to return to the Old Normal. There will be a call for change and an attempt to fill it with some very odd fads, with notions of the Orient, visions of the Tarot, and even bizarrely with an 'Angelic Flights' death cult.

The Global Federation will start when nine countries agree to pool their resources and set up a United Cross Management organisation. This will rapidly evolve as other governments see its growth, development and potential and in time, it will take over the duties and responsibilities of the UN. It will rapidly come to an awareness that the Global Federation's prime responsibility will be to prepare us for the World Government, and that it will be possible to see a Global Authority in operation by the end of the century. Yuval Harari near the beginning of the twenty-first century, felt that it was too early to be thinking of anything like that, but that if we put our minds to it and make the radical changes that are necessary and are prepared to focus on the goal, we will not only achieve and make it work but succeed in transforming our planet in the foreseeable future.

This will be regarded by some as a utopian project but unless we are prepared to think in these terms, we will get sucked back into the old ways, and we could actually lose another hundred years with our dithering ways.

I have some doubts that what I have proposed will happen in the next eighty years, as I feel it is not possible to guarantee or predict the future with great detail or accuracy, but I do believe that the time will come when we need to look for a working attendance to the UN, along the lines of the Global Federation. So, I would like to set down some proposals for the Global Federation, in the early years of its existence.

1. I feel that it should be set up as a Crisis Management Force to deal with the international crises and difficulties, to prepare for the crises that are coming at us with increasing regularity.

2. It will organise a Universal Resource Archive, so that it will be aware of the resources that are unavailable to us when the crises come and ensure that each country has its own archive.

3. It will begin work to ensure that all are fed and sheltered, that basic health systems are set up and introduce a basic, universal educational system around the globe.

4. Set up a two-army defence system: peace making (army) and peace protection (police), which will be a much more proactive force.

5. Organise a referendum on a Universal Auxiliary Language, which will be introduced as countries join the Global Federation.

6. It will organise an Emergency Adult Volunteer Force and a Youth Volunteer Force, to help with rebuilding and reorganising in distressed countries

7. It will help to organise the return of migrants and see that they are safely settled. It will not force those who do not

want to return home; it will organise settlements in third countries that are willing to take them in.

8. It will organise and set up annual World Fairs, to show new inventions and products in different countries worldwide.

9. To ensure that there is a free and democratic system, available to all with an annual report on justice and development from each country in the federation.

Depending on its success and development, it will move on to reorganise the World Bank, the World Health Organisation, the World Court and trade organisations, take over from the UN and prepare for the World Government, which will hopefully take over at the end of this century.

It is our hope that the World Government will be prepared and ready to take over as we move into the new century. No doubt, there will be attempts to delay the process but it would not be blocked or halted. When the day finally arrives, we will see the emergence of the Unity of the Species.

This will give us the chance to start the next chapter of the human story, with a new identity as Homo Evolvus. We will have a new vision, a fresh agenda and a plan to achieve it, with back up from political, scientific and religious sources. We will move into the new era with a renewed self confidence and the opportunity to realise our potential. If we start to backslide, we have no one to blame but ourselves. I have the confident belief however, that we will take the opportunity offered to us and find that we will achieve more than we ever believed was possible.

Section Two

~ The Six Levels ~

Chapter Four

The Individual

The world must seem a very strange place when we are born. It takes us a considerable time to settle in and become consciously aware of what is happening. Slowly, we begin to recognise our parents and other members of our family. Gradually, we come to know and accept a widening circle of friends, neighbours and relatives, as well as those we come into contact with on a daily basis. As we grow and develop, we come to realise that the world has a number of very different aspects, which we experience in very different ways: namely, the material, the spiritual, the emotional and the intellectual. We soon discover that we are expected to come to terms with all four if we are to develop into fully functioning human beings.

The American psychologist Andrew Maslow put it very perceptively when he identified a special hierarchy of needs for the individual. He drew up a pyramid of these needs, with food and shelter at the base level. Above this, he put safety and protection. Higher, we have the need for recognition and love. Then we have the need for esteem and appreciation. These are what Maslow describes as our primary needs and desires. Above these we have the need for 'self actualisation'. Maslow associated this with 'the peak experience'. Later, Maslow added another goal – the need for 'self transcendence'. This state is when we seek to fulfil structural goals and share altruistically.

The English writer, Colin Wilson became fascinated by the peak experience while he was writing a biography about Maslow, and he described his own last book, *Super Consciousness* as a quest for the peak experience, which he came to believe was the key to our evolutionary development. Unfortunately, Wilson died before he was able to explain this clearly or describe how it worked. So, we are not quite sure how far he had travelled on his evolutionary journey, or even how far he had developed.

At present, most of us work and live at well below our potential and only come at all close to the peak experience on very rare occasions. For myself, I think I have only touched this kind of experience on one occasion. This happened a long time ago when I was in my late teens. One evening in late autumn, I was out walking in the Dublin mountains, up a laneway towards a beautiful orange sunset. I was suddenly overwhelmed by a tremendous surge of what felt like electric energy. This came up through my feet, legs and body, passing up through my neck, head and skull. Then it was out and away. I felt, for the few moments that it passed through me, as though I knew everything I needed and wanted to know, that there were no questions I could not answer and that I had been touched by something special. This feeling only lasted for a few moments and then, I was back to where I had started, in the everyday world. When things returned to normal there was only the memory but I never forgot what had happened. It is very possible that it had just been a quirk of my imagination. I tried to repeat it on several occasions but never managed to come anywhere near the feeling and sensation again.

I think that we seriously underestimate what we can do or think, as individuals or together and that we undervalue ourselves over and over again. William James put it very succinctly, in one of the most perceptive essays he ever wrote, *On Vital Reserves,* when he suggested that we only use a small part of what is available to us physically and spiritually, because we simply do not realise the resources we possess, or how to use them. I think that most of us use little more than five per cent of the potential we have at our disposal. This is one of the great lessons that we will learn in the next eight years.

At present, there are a few exceptions. Some of us have natural abilities in different fields, while others are wonderfully adaptable. This allows them to work wonders with very little training. However, I think there are a very few geniuses around and I am sure that most of us could do a great deal more with a little help and encouragement. Even the handicapped should be given the opportunity to do as much as they can, and they can be seen in sporting events like the Paralympic Games.

I think that it is instructive to watch the golfer, Rory McIlroy at his best. According to reports, he began to take an interest in playing the game when he was only four years old, after watching his father play. He was encouraged, helped and tutored from a very early age and has developed into a world class player, even though he still has his off days. Yehudi Menuhin found that he had a talent for playing the violin when he was very young, while Martin Magill discovered a talent for public speaking after hearing his father give addresses at public meetings, while the Dalai Lama was chosen at birth, and groomed as a spiritual leader in Tibet. What I am suggesting here, is that children should be encouraged from a very early age, not forced or coerced, but helped by their parents to discover their talents.

Some people may feel that by doing this, we are robbing children of their childhood, but it is possible to do this in a balanced way. My own father loved to read bedside stories to us when we were growing up. He started by telling wild and very woolly stories, which I think he made up. When my brother and I were a little older, he introduced us to adventure stories in books like *Treasure Island, Kidnapped, The Gorilla Hunters* and *The Swiss Family Robinson.* He introduced us to poetry by reading and reciting the nonsense verses in *Alice in Wonderland* and the crazy rhymes of Edward Lear. Later, we had the rolling ballads of Robert Service about Desperate Dan McGrew and Sam McGee.

I loved these stories and poems and have been an avid reader since my teens. Since my retirement, I have managed to write four books, including two of poetry. They were so long in coming that I call them 'delayed benefit'.

Children in Ireland and in most other countries are indoctrinated, and brought up in their parents' religion from infancy, and become believers and devotees in their early teens. I feel that they should be encouraged to look at and discover the other belief systems and religions that are around. If we do not do this, we can become blinkered and behind in so much that is happening around us. The same is true in the political arena, with some adults believing that a particular brand of politics is written in their DNA. No doubt, if they had been born in another country and brought up in the prevailing religion, they would have followed it with equal fervour. We should be free to investigate and question the truth and falsehood of the received ideas and beliefs of those around us. As an old man once said to me, "They can't all be right, but they could all be wrong."

It is important to realise that we should be free to have our own beliefs, opinions and values, as long as they do not endanger or threaten others. We should be free to develop our own personality and talent, but it is important to understand and recognise that we are not only individuals but that we are also social beings, with parts to play in the world around us. We need to be able to balance our roles with those of others and accept that they have as much right from their own perspectives as we have from ours.

In the big decisions we make with others, we sometimes have to sacrifice our interests for those of the common good. Unfortunately, we are more often inclined to think and emphasise 'me' rather than 'we'. Margaret Thatcher, when she was the British Prime Minister, gave an interview in which she said that she did not believe that there was such a thing as society, and that there were only individuals. This ideal still prevails in some quarters, which go to great lengths to emphasise greed and self-interest, rather than need. No doubt, the individual is important, but we have to accept that the single individual is only one of eight billion building blocks that go to make up our global society. We will only begin to understand our potential strength and value when we all have the opportunity to play a part in building a whole new world for ourselves.

I have no doubt that some individuals, communities and nations will want to opt out of this arrangement, so that they can pursue their own ends or visions. That will be their choice and option. No doubt, they will change their tune when they see the project up and running. As they say, nothing succeeds like success.

As far as I can see, there are six different levels in the new global community that we are laying the foundations for today. You are probably vaguely aware of most of these already.

At the base level, we have the individual. I believe that each of us has a useful and valuable part to play. There will be room and a special place for all of us in this project. In time, we will all be given an opportunity to realise and fulfil our potential.

At the second level, we will have the intimate community. This is where we will find our nearest and dearest, our families and friends. These are the people who will nourish and teach us until we are ready to play our part in the wider community.

At the third level, we have the local community. In this group we will find the doctors, counsellors, teachers and workers, who help us to operate on an everyday level in the world around us.

At the next level, we have the national community. At present, this is regarded as the most important level in the whole system. Here, we find the people who run the countries that we live in and do their best to see that the place is run smoothly. At this level, we vote for deputies to represent us in national assemblies.

At the next level, we have regional communities. At present, the most obvious example is the European community or the European Union (EU). This is the most recent and successful example since the United States was formed almost two hundred and fifty years ago. It kept the states together, even after a civil war. However, the EU will move forward beyond the nation state into a regional union. At present, it does its best to guide twenty-seven nation states across Europe, making laws that affect all of its members, and making vague noises about a wider, more embracing union, with an army, a constitution and a president. However, it is still having trouble bringing the members together as a cohesive group and becoming a true union.

At the top level, we have the United Nations, doing its best to bring us all together, with little real power or success. It is brushed aside by the larger national states and is only used when it serves their purposes or meets their needs. However, it will be replaced later in this century by a Global Federation. This will have a democratic mandate to deal with our most difficult and pressing problems and crises. This is where it will start, but its main purpose will be to prepare the globe for world government and the unification of mankind – The Unity of the Species.

Each of these six levels has its own particular part to play, and each of them will be important in its own way, though we do not quite appreciate this yet. We will not realise our potential until we have the six levels working smoothly together, performing their own particular duties and accepting their place in the system. I have no doubt that this is what will happen. I also have no doubt that some individuals and communities will look back to the good old days with nostalgia and affection, when the world was a very different place but as the Buddha said, "This too will pass."

Chapter Five

The Intimate Community

I am writing here about those who are closest to us. By this, I mean our families, friends, neighbours, relations, teachers and those we work and live with on a day-to-day basis. These are the people who usually have the greatest influence on us, from a very early age. They introduce us to the world and the different ways of seeing, knowing and doing things. Our memories of them and the lessons that they teach us lodge in our minds and often resonate with us for the rest of our lives.

Unfortunately, they are also responsible for many of the lies and misguided beliefs that clog up our systems. Ideas that somehow become part of our DNA, or so we come to imagine. This can cause us to believe and act in peculiar and unreasonable ways, especially when it comes to certain subjects like politics, religion, history, geography, money and sex.

Many of the beliefs that we have are simply myths, legends and superstitions, which we often hold on to with passion and accept as verifiable truth. When we examine these stories and beliefs carefully, we often come to realise that they make little or no sense, with absolutely nothing of any substance to support them. We are told that something is true, even when it is prejudice, gossip or mangled nonsense. This is how so many stories about flying saucers, folktales about fairies and witches, religious and scientific myths, and historic yarns have developed, grown and blossomed into unquestionable truths, faith and facts.

Perhaps I can best explain this by describing how I was introduced to this strange, changing and evolving world. I grew up in a traditional, middle-class, Irish Catholic family in suburban Dublin during the middle years of the last century. We were taught at school that our Catholic faith was our most precious possession, and that it was our first duty to pass it on to the next generation.

I did question some of our religious beliefs and practices, as well as the cultural norms that we were brought up with at the Christian Brothers school where I was educated. I carried many of the beliefs and customs into my adult life before I left home to live in Britain in my early twenties.

At school, I found it difficult to understand why the Christian Brothers, who believed in a caring Saviour, Jesus Christ, and the power of love and confession, ruled us with the fear of God and the power of a thick, leather strap. As Christian Brothers, they emphasised the power of repetition and the importance of following orders. They were reasonably effective in their methods, but they seldom encouraged us to think for ourselves. For instance, I found it difficult to understand why we had to learn Gaelic, the Irish language. This is still regarded as the national and first official language in Ireland. As far as I can see, English is perfectly adequate for communications, and most of us here in Ireland use English rather than Irish in our daily lives. I came away from school, after learning Gaelic for ten years, with only a smattering of the Irish language. Oddly enough, I can still rattle off a couple of prayers in Gaelic after sixty years.

Shortly after leaving school, I went to live in England, where I met up with Peter Gill at the Church Army Hostel in Oxford. We became firm friends and travelled round the country together for some time. He brought me down to Torquay in Devon for a summer season. Torquay is a lively holiday resort, which I fell in love with on my first night there. We stayed in the town for almost three years. I really felt at home there and came to regard it as my spiritual home. While we were there, Peter introduced me to the Bahá'í Movement, which later became the Bahá'í Faith. I knew a little about some of the other religions beyond Christianity but I had never heard of Bahá'í before. I liked the sound of it when I heard of its principles. One of these was 'The Independent Investigation of Truth'. I appreciated this, so did Peter. It really struck a chord with me and attracted me to take a close look at the movement.

Bahá'í brought me to meet my present wife, Anne. She has been my constant companion and helpmate for the last fifty years, and has always been a marvellous support, though we have our ups and downs.

What I remember best about Peter was his questioning spirit. I soon realised that he seemed to question absolutely everything, or so it seemed to me. He asked questions about the British monarchy, about the need to play the national anthem after public events. He questioned the need to work and the value of money. He wondered about the way we dressed, and why women wore make up. He was critical of the television news and why we seemed to accept it all. He asked why we believed the most absurd things in religion and politics, and why we needed armies and artists. He asked so many questions, and he sometimes got into ridiculous trouble by asking the wrong questions at the wrong time, so I had to move away from him. I had never met anyone who had used a version of the Socratic method and approach in his daily life. I was impressed, though his questions sometimes got us into a lot of unnecessary trouble.

Today I believe that we should not accept whatever we have been told, from even the most reliable sources, until we have had a chance to examine and test for ourselves. I have come to appreciate the value of critical and negative thinking. If you look closely, you will see that so many ideas, beliefs and stories that we heard and accepted are often changed, distorted, embellished and misunderstood before they reach our ears. When you think about it, this is probably how so many things change, develop and evolve from one generation to the next, in good ways and bad. Not only this but it is very possibly how so many of our collective beliefs about gays, single mothers, the handicapped, immigrants, art, architecture, and even the way we think and express ourselves and work have evolved out of all recognition, during the past hundred years. When I was growing up, homosexuals, lesbians and transexuals were despised, imprisoned, ridiculed and laughed at, because of their unconventional ways. Today, in many countries, these practices are regarded as perfectly normal and a matter of choice. Many of these so-called deviants are married in civil ceremonies and even manage to become prime ministers in some places. It is only a matter of time before euthanasia and other contentious policies will be accepted and approved in even conservative countries.

The goalposts have certainly been moved in some respects. In the not-so-distant past, women were widely regarded as second-class citizens, and still are in some Muslim countries of the Middle East, though there are clear signs that, before the end of the century, the equality of men and women will be universally accepted and observed. It is strange to think that women had to give up their jobs when they got married, and that single women who got pregnant were often obliged to go into special homes to have their babies. It is very notable that, in the sphere of crime and punishment, attempted suicides could result in fines or imprisonment, while debtors had their own special prisons and the unemployed had to go into workhouses. While today young people often live together for some time, have babies and buy houses before they think of getting married, the middle-aged go back to college and a job for life is becoming a rarity.

I was particularly struck and amused when I was sitting in a doctor's waiting room recently. I saw a woman with a small child on her lap. The young one was sucking a soother while it played with the woman's mobile phone. When I looked over a short time later, the woman and the infant were playing a simple game of 'pass the parcel' with a clutch of the woman's credit and debit cards. I may be overstating it, but it seemed to me that I was watching evolution in action. It appeared that the woman was introducing the child to computers and the digital revolution, before the child could talk.

I wonder who is going to introduce us to evolution in a clearer and more focussed way than at present. Which of our parents, teachers, philosophers or politicians will show us how the process works creatively in practice? Are we going to have to pick up the information, as we do today, in a haphazard and unfocussed way? We certainly use evolution in a better and more informed way than we did before Darwin came up with his theories, but could we use it in a wiser and more precise way? I think that if we used it properly, it could help to prepare us for what is coming and enable us to deal with the problems and crises as they come up. We are beginning to understand this in our approach to Climate Change, but it is obvious that we could do a great deal more, and we will when we have a greater appreciation of what is happening.

I believe that evolution will be taught as a subject at our colleges and universities. This could be introduced initially at summer schools in the next few years, and I am surprised that this has not happened yet. This workbook has been written to help and encourage the process. I think that it will be unfortunate and a real pity if we miss the opportunity to move forward. No doubt, there are other options, which I would love to hear about. If we miss this chance, and repeat the mistakes of the last century, it is possible that we may have to wait another hundred years before we become aware of the radical and significant changes that are coming, and that evolution will bring in, eventually.

Chapter Six

The Local Community

As far as I can see, the Local Community is one of the most undervalued resources that we have today. When we can see and understand how to use it, it will undoubtedly change and improve out of all recognition.

The Local Community is the essential link between the Intimate and National Communities, dealing with our everyday needs, requirements and the way we conduct our business on a basic, social level. Aspiring politicians often use urban and rural councils, which are the political channels of the local community, as an entry point, before they go on to work at national level. These councils offer a wide variety of services to meet the community needs. These include providing transport, parks, roads, planning, housing, water, education, libraries, fire and health services, as well as assisting business and community groups. Political parties have not been slow to realise the value of local networking, and have organised at a local level, serving on the councils to forward their own ends. They have undoubtedly found this very useful, but it can distort community value, at times, in order to serve their own interests.

Too often we are not aware of what is happening at council meetings and behind the scenes. Social media pays a good deal more attention to what is happening at national level than the local, which is understandable but unfortunate. Recently, public participation forums have been introduced in some countries, to facilitate greater participation and awareness by ordinary citizens with local bodies but so far, this reception has been ambivalent and muffled at that. However, the attitude will change after Climate Change hits us. This will cause wholesale damage, destruction and devastation on an unprecedented scale. One of the most interesting and engaging signs of change will be the appearance of the Hubs. This is an initiative that will come from Germany. Hubs will be adopted by many European cities and towns and will become a common feature of our social landscape and way of life.

In their earliest phase, these circular buildings will be used by local councils as work centres, and for government business but slowly, their remit will focus, develop and widen communications. Each of these Hubs will contain a number of offices, and two or three sizeable halls. Closest to the entrance, on the left-hand side, will be the Ombudsman's office, where ordinary people can bring complaints, grievances and difficulties. Next to this, we will have the Local Resources Centre and Work Offices. While on other side of the aisle, we will have the Local Administrative Offices and Research and Development Department, where the future of the area will be planned and mapped out.

A central corridor leads to two halls. In one, the everyday business of the council will be conducted, while the other will be used to host public service exhibitions, a cafe and a number of video rooms, where there will be regular showings, and even a third hall for public forums and for presentation awards. This Hub will be a truly public centre, which will do its best to inform, explain and entertain and if possible, to get people to become involved in running their own community.

The Hubs will come in various sizes to meet the needs and requirements of particular communities. They will expand, grow and develop over a number of years, and in time become the central focus of new towns and cities.

Originally, they come down from the ideas and suggestions of the American inventor and evolutionist, Jacque Fresco, and the videos that he made of his Venus Project in Florida, before they were taken up and developed in Germany. As Fresco pictured it, the Hubs would be the central power houses of the towns and cities. His Hubs contain the computers and equipment that will run the world around them and gradually evolve, with the vision and insights of innumerable individuals and communities.

I am writing here from the perspective of the highly developed First World. The pace of change will be slower on other levels, but later in this century it will ramp up. By the end of this period, all areas will be roughly similar, as the globe evolves into a world state. If it does not develop quite like this and we are still bickering, fighting and competing, it will mean that we want to progress at a slower pace and possibly put real change back. I sincerely hope that we do not make the same mistakes that we made in the last century and that we try to make a better world for our children. We can start this by making a more progressive life for ourselves in the Intimate and Local Communities.

Chapter Seven

The National Community

In our world today, the National Community plays a pre-eminent part in political affairs, which is unfortunate to say the least. Looking around us at home and abroad, the National Community seems to be the only show in town, from a political and practical point of view.

At a regional and a global level, attempts have been made to change this, to provide a counterbalancing authority. They have only been partially successful at best. On a regional level, we have seen the emergence of the European community, while on a global level we have the United Nations, both of which have put in an appearance since the Second World War. However, the nation states have kept a tight control of matters and neither of the new organs managed to reach their full potential. We have the larger members at the national level band together, to try and keep unruly states in order, while they sideline the UN. It became clear that unless something happened, that the UN would become a seriously dysfunctional body.

Nation states go back over a thousand years in one form or another, and some believe that they have been in existence since the foundation of Islam, in the 7th century AD. Most of these states have had sovereign rulers up to the end of the 18th century, when we saw a slow changeover to voting democracies, especially in Europe and America. This form of government has become the standard model on the continents. Today there are over two hundred democratic states, a dwindling string of sovereign nations and a shrinking number of dictators spread across the globe.

National democratic governments have served the world reasonably well though, from the start, they have competed with each other, and the successful ones have spent a considerable time empire-building overseas. This has been a reoccurring problem, which came to a head in the twentieth century, when the national model began to show signs of strain and weakness.

This exploded with the madness of the First World War, which saw forty million people die needlessly. This war had a sobering effect of sorts and saw the emergence of the League of Nations. It was formed to ensure that the horror would not be repeated, and that it would keep the belligerent nations apart. The League was only a partial success. It managed to keep the fighting nations at a safe distance but only for twenty years.

Then we had a Second World War, which came like a sequel to the first. This was an even more ferocious and destructive conflict, with many of the same contestants involved. When they finally signed off on this war, with a bomb to end all bombs, which had the power to exterminate all life on Earth, one would have thought that we would have learned our lesson and taken radical action, which would ensure this kind of thing never happened again. There was a flurry of activity, and I think we really believed that we were doing the right thing when we set up the United Nations. This managed to keep an uneasy peace for the next hundred years but by the fourth decade of the 21st century, it will become obvious that the UN had become a dysfunctional body, which had been adequate in the twentieth century, but that we needed a proactive force to meet the challenges of the twenty-first.

As the world will not be quite ready for a world government and a New World Order, it will be suggested that we need a Global Federation, which will look after our present international problems, difficulties and crises with a more proactive agenda and authority than the UN possessed. However, it will not make its appearance until after Climate Change and the migration that followed. Then we will be ready to take the radical action required.

Chapter Eight

The Regional Community

Regional communities come in different shapes and sizes. Here, I am writing about those states that have come together to form larger communities, rather than small areas or counties that are part of a larger country. The US is a good example of where the States came together and managed to form a United States of America, while the Union of Soviet Socialist Republics is an example of a not-so-successful unification project.

In the past, the European powers were particularly good at power grabbing. The English, Portuguese, Spanish and Dutch were all very adept at collecting colonies, settlements and satellites in Africa, South America and the Middle and Far East. Interestingly enough, the English formed a United Kingdom with England, Scotland, Wales and Ireland as its constituent parts, while Russia came late to the game with the USSR, as it roped a cluster of Eastern European States after the Second World War. However, it was forced to give up the project when communism slipped off the rails towards the end of the twentieth century, though the Russian attempt at power grabbing in neighbouring Ukraine showed that nationalist violence is still alive and active in the twenty-first century.

Perhaps the most positive and forward-looking political development at the regional level since the Second World War, has been the appearance of the European Economic Community, which is now known as the European Union. Its long-term goal was to unite the European states, bringing them together economically and politically, something along the lines of what

Americans achieved after their Civil War. There were six European countries in this regional community at the beginning: namely Belgium, France, Germany, Italy, Luxembourg and the Netherlands. The founders hoped that the proposed union would increase between the member states and promote peace, so that there would be no further wars between the neighbouring countries of Europe. It has certainly worked well, up to a point, and brought peace and stability to the people of Europe.

In 1988, its name was changed to the European Union (EU). The Community has grown, developed and prospered since it was formed after the Second World War, and the number of states in the community has increased to twenty-seven. It will grow even larger when a number of European countries join. Of course, it has had its problems and difficulties, but there is no sign of the community breaking down. So far, only Britain has dropped out. The Russia-Ukraine war offered a timely reminder of what could happen in Europe if war returned.

The question we need to ask is a simple one. What next? It has been suggested that we could see a United States of Europe, with a president, a constitution and a regional army. So far, we do not seem to be ready for a move like this, but it will come eventually.

The EU has been a great help to Europe, by promoting trade on the continent and as a peacekeeper but the world needs a stronger and more proactive authority than the United Nations. This is the role that will be taken by the Global Federation, as we move towards a multinational Global Community. This is the area I would like to work at next.

Chapter Nine

The Global Community

The closest we have come to creating a global community was when we set up the United Nations at the end of the Second World War. A charter of the United Nations (UN) was signed on 25 June 1945, in San Francisco. On that date, forty-five nations gathered for the first ever conference of the new organisation, which was billed as 'a gathering of peace-loving nations', though it would be more accurate to describe it as a conference of the allied victors of the Second World War, as it was led and guided by the US, who hoped that the new organisation would do what the predecessor, the League of Nations, had not been able to do: namely, keep the peace between the belligerent European powers.

The UN was certainly a more robust organisation than the League of Nations, and it managed to ensure that we have not had a Third World War for the better part of a century, though we did come close once or twice. It grew, developed and managed to embrace over two hundred nation states around the world. It also managed to foster a considerable number of valuable and useful global agencies. These included the World Bank, a world court in the form of the International Court of Justice, the World Health Organisation and a world peacekeeping force. However, the two main bodies of the United Nations, since its inception, have been the Security Council and the General Assembly. The more powerful of the two being the Security Council. This, more often than not, reflects the conflicting views of the Great Powers: namely, the US and its transatlantic allies on the one hand, and the Russian and Chinese governments on the other.

Meanwhile, the General Assembly offered a forum for the different states of all hues to air their views and opinions on all subjects, but little more.

Since it was set up, the UN has played a part in many of the international hot and cool conflicts on the world stage, as a mediator and a peacekeeper. Unfortunately, it has not been able to stop the major powers fighting and killing in Korea, Vietnam, Yugoslavia, Afghanistan and Ukraine. Meanwhile it has been active as a mediator between the Arabs and Israelis in Israel for over fifty years, without a satisfying result.

While the organisation has worthwhile aspirations and noble ideas, it has not been able to act as a fully functioning global authority. It seems that thus far, the major powers are reluctant to move forward, relinquish some of their power and authority and put their trust in an independent international body.

Some time ago, the UN produced a plan with seventeen sustainable goals. These cover economic and social targets, which offer benchmarks for commitment at corporate and national levels. This project and others seem to be blocked by the veto of the permanent members of the security council.

The UN charter requires that all members of the Security Council agree before substantial action is taken. The sad but inescapable truth is that the UN continues to be sidelined by the Great Powers, who use the veto for their own particular purposes.

Things will only begin to change when Climate Change and migrational crises hit us. Then we will hear urgent calls for meaningful action but even then, we would not see substantial action, until we experience the Last Great War, with its nuclear devastation. Then we will begin to see decisive action on a number of fronts to bring about radical change. Then we will see the Global Federation come into existence, following the Rome Conference of 2055. Its chief architect will be the Italian philosopher Mario Rossi. He had written a book called simply, *The Global Federation* and will propose that we set up a Voluntary Crises Force to deal with the series of crises and problems that we will be faced with. He will propose that we need to pool our resources and work together as a global community, in a focussed and structured way. His work will attract the attention of a small group of European governments, who will organise the Rome Conference. There will be fifty countries at the first significant conference, and they will agree that we must only look forward but that we need to do something about it. They will agree that we must work in a determined way, laying aside our natural and personal differences and strangely enough, this is what they will do.

In the following decade, the Global Federation will come into being. It will move through a number of changes, from the Federation, the International Council, towards Global Authority and on to the World Government at the end of the century. The pace of change will be slow to start with but will come with considerable fanfare. It will be fast and furious at times and arrive with a constitution and a world president at the turn of the century.

I think we will be genuinely surprised at how much we will achieve, working together as One People, as Yuval Harari suggested, "Humans rose to dominate the planet, not simply because they were more clever or intelligent, but because they learnt how to cooperate, and they proved better at this than their cousins, the Neanderthals".

When we come together, I think we will realise that we have the opportunity to choose our path to the future, as we take our next evolutionary step.

If we are prepared to finally sink our differences and work together in a structured, cooperative and peaceful way, guided by a democratic world authority, with an outward, future-looking agenda and a fresh set of goals, we will turn this world into a powerhouse, and a place where we can all realise our potential.

Just think of it, we will have a fresh agenda, which will encourage us to investigate the worlds within and without, and then be prepared to share our findings. We will travel to other planets and galaxies. We will be able to use evolution in creative, proactive and reactive ways to make the world a better place for all of us.

We will investigate the fourth, fifth and sixth dimensions. We will interface and work with AI, and aliens when we can find them. We will have a Universal Auxiliary Language, which will help us to understand others. We will be able to use telepathy, hypnotism and meditation in extraordinary ways. We will have a Universal House of Justice to guide and advise us, with a constitutional Book of Laws. I could go on and on, but this is just the beginning of a new age that we are about to enter, and the Unity will soon come in sight. Who knows where or how far evolution will take us? But it is ours to invent.

Section Three

~ Evolution and Evolutionists ~

Chapter Ten

The Evolutionary Shift: Shaping our Future

Evolution is a process in which organisms change, develop and evolve over time to become more suited and better able to cope with their environments. We only seem to have become aware of the importance of evolution since Darwin wrote his ground-breaking study, *On the Origin of Species*, in the middle of the nineteenth century, following his travels around the Galapagos islands in the Pacific and his close study of the animals and birds that he found there. In a number of the books that he wrote after returning home, he offered the theory that biological evolution worked through a process of natural selection, and that it was driven by a primal urge – 'the survival of the fittest'.

Since Darwin's time, the Theory of Evolution has itself evolved, and we have a broader perspective now, finding the process at work in a wide variety of fields. This can be seen most obviously in some of our technological inventions and innovations, like cars, planes and computers. Over time, they have been transformed, and decade by decade, they have evolved to meet our needs and requirements.

The evolutionists who followed Darwin have seen evolution at work in many strange, useful and productive ways. For instance, Colin Wilson looked at it from the perspective of individual consciousness. Teilhard de Chardin used it in his cosmic speculations. Richard Dawkins revered it in a scientific fundamentalist way, and for his theory of 'cultural memes'.

Mirza Hussein Ali AKA Bahá'u'lláh used it in the religious sphere, and as an essential block for his new religion. Tim Smit adopted it to blend past, present and future in his eco-project, the Eden Project, while Jacque Fresco used it in his YouTube videos and H.G. Wells used it to fuel his science fiction. While Darwin looked back, so many of the evolutionists looked forward, to show where evolution could take us in the future.

In the past century, we have come up with some marvellous inventions and innovations. We have made great strides in health care and life management. We have created fabulous buildings, monuments and megacities but in so many ways, our social lives still look back to the good old days of the twentieth century, and this is where evolution will help in the future.

As far as I can see, evolution is about more than change and progress. What it can do is register the changes that occur, and that we make. By consulting and working with it, we can gauge and measure, change, eradicate and make progress. Evolution can do this on a small or grand scale, registering the changes that we make, as we move through the portals into the New World Order. At present, we are in the process of making an evolutionary shift, moving from the technological into the Unity revolution.

Today, we do not need 'deep time' to register the changes that are happening and that we are making. The pace of change means that the time between these evolutionary shifts is growing shorter and at the same time, we are becoming more aware of what is happening. We are able to take notes and record or register it more carefully. Most of the time, we realise that something is happening, but more often than not, we do not know what. Some of us know more than others and these are often the evolutionists who are our guides and mapmakers to the future world. Occasionally, they go down blind alleys, but they often give us glimpses of what is coming up and even how we should get there.

I have been asked why I think we are moving into the Unity revolution at this stage, while the awesome, technological revolution is still at full throttle and we still have many lessons to learn from it. There are a number of very good reasons why it is the coming Unity revolution and not something else. I can think of at least five good reasons why.

(1) Unity will benefit us all, not just one particular group, one sector, or part of humanity. As Bahá'u'lláh said, "The world is one country, and mankind are its citizens."

This seems to hit the point. We need to see and be aware of our common ownership of the globe.

(2) It is going to bring us closer together. We can and should be able to face our problems together. We will be able to deal with them more easily, pool our resources and tackle them in a focussed and more structured way.

(3) Because it will help us to realise our potential, as individuals, communities and a species.

(4) Because it will give us a chance to make a fresh start, with a new vision and agenda for the next century.

(5) Because it meets the zeitgeist, the need for Unity. If there is something more pertinent I would certainly like to hear of it.

Chapter Eleven

The Evolutionists

In this section I would like to look at a very special group, whom I call the evolutionists. These are the individuals who have most influenced my thinking about the process of evolution. Here, I want to concentrate on the main players, from Darwin onwards, who have opened out the debate about the theory. Evolution seems to mean different things to different people and I am certain that a considerable number of those whom I have included, have had no idea that they have been involved in the debate about evolution.

Many of Darwin's followers have looked forward to the future and speculated on what evolution can tell us about what is coming, from different perspectives. In this, many of them align themselves with the futurists, who are simply interested in predicting and foretelling what they believe the future will offer us.

Evolution is rather like some of the great religions, such as Christianity and Islam. They usually started off with an individual prophet and his teachings. Today, the stories of these prophets and their beliefs have evolved into the world's great religions. Looking around, one can see innumerable groups, sects, cults and heresies that have grown from different interpretations of their founders' lives and work. Evolution is very similar, though only Dawkins and Bahá'u'lláh have sought to turn their findings and beliefs into modern-day religions.

I find it fascinating to see how different people and groups have responded to the Theory of Evolution, and to realise that our collective response to it could possibly shape the way we think, feel, believe and respond in the future, as we shift and evolve from Homo Sapiens to Homo Evolvus.

Here I must admit that I am sorry that there is only one woman, and a very young one at that, Greta Thunberg, amongst my evolutionists. No doubt, there will be many more included in future editions of this work. At least, I certainly hope so.

Charles Darwin

Charles Darwin, the father of evolutionary studies, was born on 12 February 1809 in Shrewsbury, England. His father, Robert Darwin, was a respected and wealthy family doctor. Charles went to Edinburgh University, where he studied Medicine, before he changed to Divinity. However, his real interest was in Natural History.

At college, he was influenced by Robert Grant, an evolutionary thinker, with whom he went on a number of field trips. He became a close friend of the Rev John Henshaw, who recommended him as a naturalist and companion to James Fitzroy, Master of the *HMS Beagle*. This certainly appealed much more to Darwin than taking on a small country parish as a rural clergyman.

Although his father did not approve, Darwin sailed off on the *Beagle* on an expedition round the Pacific, stopping for some time to explore the primeval forests of Brazil and the foothill of the Andes, before he arrived at the volcanic islands of the Galapagos archipelago. While he was there, Darwin had a wonderful opportunity to make an intensive study of the fossils and wildlife on the different islands of the chain. He was very impressed by the giant turtle that he found there, but he became engaged and almost obsessed when he discovered some similar but radically different animals and birds living on the various islands. When he examined the creatures more closely, he came to the conclusion that the different species had changed when they moved from one island to another.

It was during this period that his revolutionary theories for the book, *On the Origin of Species* were born, grew and evolved. In this book, the idea of natural selection was born and developed. He came to the conclusion that through the process of natural selection, different species could preserve favourable variations in different settings. The principle underlying this theory was that no species was immutable, all had evolved and continued to do so, through long periods of time, This is a process that is called 'deep time'. Darwin further speculated that animals descended from at most, four or five progenitors. This challenged the prevailing idea that the different species had all been specifically and selectively created.

When he came back to England from his travels, Darwin was entirely reluctant and very slow to publicise his findings about evolution, which he thought would upset and threaten a number of the scientific and religious views of the time. It took him over twenty years before he was able to publish *On the Origin of Species* in November 1859.

The book was a surprisingly popular bestseller, and its author became a household name and a national celebrity. Essentially, what happened over a short period of time, was that Darwin had revolutionised society's understanding of the natural world around us and allowed us to see it in a new way. Strangely enough, for all Darwin's brilliant insights into the origin of ants, birds and other living creatures, he had almost nothing to say about Homo Sapiens in his first book. He made only a passing reference in *On the Origin of Species*.

Towards the end of the work, he referred to the light that will be shed on the origin of mankind and history. This was all that he was prepared to say at that point about the origin of the single most important species on the planet. He felt that he would have to find more evidence before he was prepared to publish his findings.

Twelve years later, in 1871, he felt safe enough to bring out another book, *The Descent of Man*, that was devoted to this particular subject. Although it is not as familiar as *On the Origin of Species,* it has a great deal more to say about the biological implications of Darwin's theories

In *The Descent of Man*, he argues that all living beings belong to one species, and that all races come down to a single ancestral base. He went on to point out that there were considerable similarities between early humans and apes. He concluded by suggesting that chimps and gorillas were very possibly our closest living relatives. He then suggested that, given the relationship between them, that our earliest known ancestors probably came from Africa originally.

However, the missing link between man and ape has never been found, despite a great deal of searching and digging. There have been a few possible sightings, but none have managed to produce the evidence required. There was one notable forgery, known as 'Piltdown Man', which had the jaws of an ape and the skull of a human cleverly brought together, but this was revealed as a fake after close investigation.

Since the appearance of *On the Origin of Species*, Darwin's ideas, theories and suppositions have inspired a great deal of valuable experiment and investigation, not only in scientific fields but in other areas like literature, technology and cognitive studies, and in very many other ways that Darwin could not have possibly imagined.

Even many of the religions have come to accept many of Darwin's ideas about the evolutionary process, though some authorities in the field still have great difficulty in accepting that man has a close relationship with other species, or even that the history of humanity goes back more than five thousand years.

Today Darwin is revered as the scientist who freed us to see life from a fresh, useful and valuable perspective, and encouraged us to disregard the prejudices of the past. However, we still have a 'Theory of Evolution' rather than the 'Law of Evolution' or 'Darwin's Law' – presumably because we are still waiting for the 'missing link' to show up? Darwin's legacy has helped to show and explain to us how evolution works but in some ways, the implications of the theory are still being examined and explored, and like the reptiles on a disturbed pond, they are still being investigated by the evolutionists and others, and thankfully still offer us fresh insights in a number of fields, which will eventually take us to the Unity.

H.G. Wells

The English writer and social prophet Herbert George (Bertie) Wells was born on 21 September 1866, in the small market town of Bromley in Kent. His father owned a small delftware shop on Bromley High Street.

Wells was a clever boy who showed academic promise, but his father went bankrupt and had to give up his business. So, Wells was taken from school at thirteen and became an apprentice in a drapery store, where he had to work thirteen hours a day. He recalled this period as one of the unhappiest in his life, but he read a great deal and continued to study. A few years later, he managed to get a job as an assistant teacher at Midhurst Grammar School. Subsequently, he went on to pass a number of exams in scientific subjects and in 1884, he received a government scholarship to the Normal School of Science, South Kensington. While he was at that school, he had the good fortune to be taught Biology and Zoology by Thomas Henry Huxley.

Huxley was an affable but combative man, who was known in some circles as 'Darwin's Bulldog'. Wells had an extremely good relationship with Huxley, who once advised him to read Darwin's, *On the Origin of Species* twice. When Wells asked him why he should do this, the older man smiled and told him, "The first time is to come to an understanding of what evolution means, The second time is to understand how to use it."

Wells did not quite understand what Huxley meant, but he took this advice and found that it was well worth the trouble, using it extensively in his own writing at a later stage. He later claimed that it set him to think about the process of evolution, and how it would affect the future of mankind.

Some time after this, he suffered severe injuries to his kidneys and lungs on the playing fields of a small private school in North Wales. This forced him to give up teaching and look for another way of earning a living. He had been slowly making his way as a writer and a journalist.

In 1893, he wrote his first book, *Text-Book of Biology*, which was well received. It encouraged him to think of becoming a full-time writer. A little earlier, he had written a story about time travel called *The Chronic Argonauts*, which was published in *The Science Schools Journal*. Some time later, he redrafted the story with the help of a friend, W. E. Henley and managed to complete his first novel, *The Time Machine* in 1895. He was hopeful that it would launch his literary career and earn him some decent money.

The book was initially a modest success, which managed to earn him a hundred pounds. However, it did bring him a considerable reputation, with one reviewer even calling him a man of genius, and it is still in print today.

This first book of science fiction was followed by several others in the same vein. *The Island of Doctor Moreau* appeared in 1896, and this was followed, in quick succession, by *The Invisible Man*, *The War of the Worlds* and *The Sleeper Awakes*, which came out in 1899. All these books were well received and brought in increasing rewards. Wells was very encouraged and he realised that he had a considerable talent in producing this kind of work. He continued to write this kind of book, but he widened his approach and scope as time went by.

In the early years of the new century, the fame and popularity of his work grew. The books were translated into French, German, Spanish and Russian and he became a considerable literary figure. His earnings increased year by year, and he found this very reassuring. He moved on to write novels with contemporary themes, set in England, about his own experiences growing up. In 1902, he managed to write a book of essays about possible scientific and technological developments and he made exciting progress in the new century. This brought him into contact with the Fabian Society, one of the most important and influential literary societies in London. However, his radical socialist ideas were too much for the more prominent figures in the society, so after a while, he felt that he had to withdraw.

He even tried to move into politics in the 1920s. He stood unsuccessfully for Labour in two elections before he realised that he was not cut out for this kind of public life, and that his real forte was in writing influential books.

He was extremely productive, writing a great number of novels, essays, histories, and several booklets about the New World Order, which he believed would come into being, later in the 20th century. For most of his life, he was a vocal advocate for socialism, scientific progress, women's rights and social equality. He was not slow in putting forward controversial ideas, some of which shocked and outraged his contemporaries.

He also wrote a number of books and pamphlets in the 1930s, which warned about the Second World War and he prophesied the coming of World Government. These works include a history of the future, which he called, *The Shape of Things to Come.* In this book, he draws attention to the lessons of the Great War and hopes that we would not repeat the bout of madness, and that there will be a world authority to protect us in the future.

Wells grew increasingly depressed during the Second World War and felt that he had failed badly, because he had not been able to move the world towards his socialist utopia. He did, however, manage to write *The Rights of Man,* which is said to have inspired the foundation of the United Nations, and the important United Nations Declaration.

Bahá'u'lláh (aka Mirza Hussein Ali)

Mirza Hussein Ali, prophet, philosopher and poet was born in Tehran, capital of Iran in 1817. He was brought up as a Shia Muslim but he became a member of the Bahá'ís, a new radical religious movement, which had been started in 1844 by twenty-five-year-old Siyyid 'Alí Muḥammad, who had taken the name, the Báb (the Gate). The new movement upset the country's ruling elite, who captured and executed the Báb as a heretic, and outlawed the new movement.

Mirza Husain Ali was arrested, imprisoned and banished to Iraq, where he gradually assumed leadership of the group. He took the name of Bahá'u'lláh, which means, 'the Glory of God', and declared that the movement was now to be known as a new independent religion called 'Bahá'í'.

Bahá'u'lláh was deported from Iraq to Adrianople and later to Haifa in Israel. He lived there, under house arrest, until his death in 1896. Bahá'u'lláh spent most of his life as a prisoner, but he never tried to escape or avoid his enemies. He accepted his captivity with stoic fortitude, and he managed to transcribe and dictate over two hundred books and tablets, including, *The Seven Valleys* and *The Hidden Words,* which are still read and revered in over fifty languages today. He widened and universalised the Báb's message, and laid the foundations for a New World Order, which has its centre on Mount Carmel.

When Bahá'u'lláh died his son, Abdul Baha, took over and remained in charge of the movement for the next twenty-five years. As a senior citizen, Abdul Baha travelled extensively around Europe and the USA. In America, he aroused considerable interest and made many converts to the new religion. Bahá'í came to be regarded as a radically ambitious social movement. It championed racial and gender equality, an international auxiliary language and the formation of a world government. Abdul Baha established the Bahá'í faith on a firm basis in the United States, where he found some of his most enthusiastic followers.

While he was in America he laid the foundations of an impressive nine-sided temple in Chicago. Abdul Baha's grandson, the Oxford-educated Shoghí Effendi took over as leader and guardian of the faith in 1921. He strengthened and consolidated the administrative order of the movement and established a World Centre on the side of the holy mountain of Mount Carmel, overlooking the city of Haifa, on the Bay of Acca.

In 1963, the first democratically elected ruling body of the Bahá'ís was formed and into the middle years of this century, it had developed into the second most widely established religion after Christianity. This will change in the second half of this century as its profile develops, and it will play a significant part in world development after the Last Great War.

The stated principles of the Bahá'í faith are:

(1) The Oneness of Mankind

(2) The evolutionary nature of religion

(3) Like everything else, it grows, develops and evolves

(4) Universal education for all

(5) Equality of men and women. If there is discrimination for any reasons, it this must be explained or revised

(6) The complimentary nature of science and religion should be acknowledged. They can and should be able to work together, like the wings of a bird

(7) A democratically elected World Parliament, World Legislature and House of Justice

(8) An adequate, one-tier world health system

(9) A universal auxiliary language

(10) The abolition of prejudice and superstition.

Bahá'u'lláh wrote that the great religions have the same source and are part of an evolutionary story of mankind's structural and social development. He taught that there has been an evolving line of prophets since the beginning of time, who have brought the same spiritual message. However, their social message changes to meet the needs of the particular age, and ours is the Unity of the Species. He claimed that in the foreseeable future, we will see the unity of mankind established, materially and spiritually, guided by a democratically elected world parliament. Bahá'u'lláh left a special book, the *Kitáb-i-Aqdas*, which contains an overview of the laws and ordinances that we will need for the coming dispensation, which will last for a thousand years. He further promised that there will be another prophet, who will come to help us on the next stage of our journey.

Bahá'í has not had a particularly strong profile on the world stage, as the old age fades away, though this will undoubtedly change as we move towards the portals of the New World Order.

Bahá'í has been developing a universal educational system, with a programme that starts with some very basic lessons, which will ensure the participants receive the same basic knowledge and learning, worldwide.

Religion has not had a particularly good press for some time, due to of clerical abuse, fundamentalist violence but mainly because it is not meeting the needs of the new age. More often than not, it is regarded as being too conservative and backward looking, if not anachronistic and, at its best, it has reached its sell-by date. However, I think that it has a great deal to offer, and that it can still offer us the vision of a better world and way of life, unrivalled ethical insights and a moral code, an ability to offer us comfort and solace in time of trouble and sorrow, and it can inspire us to work miracles. God knows we certainly need that today, as we move in our own crazy way towards the Unity.

Teilhard de Chardin

The Jesuit theologian and distinguished scientist Pierre Teilhard de Chardin was born in France on 1 May 1881. His father was an enthusiastic naturalist who encouraged his family to take a keen interest in the natural world and the collection of specimens, while his mother was a conservative Catholic who awakened and strengthened his spirituality.

Teilhard was just twelve when he was sent off to Jesuit college. Seven years later, he entered a seminary at Aix-en-Provence, where he began his theological career and decided that he wanted to become a Jesuit priest. He taught physics and chemistry in Egypt before he left for England, to complete his theological studies at Hastings. He developed an interest in evolution after reading Henri Bergson's, *Creative Evolution* and came to believe that the process of evolution would take us to the eventual Unity of the Species.

Although the idea of evolution enthralled and fascinated him, he had considerable difficulty with two Darwinian concepts: Natural Selection and Survival of the Fittest, which appeared to conflict with what he had been taught as a Catholic.

From 1912 to 1914, he worked in a palaeontology laboratory in the natural history museum in Paris, studying the mammals of the Middle Tertiary Period. In 1912, he became involved with an organised digging team, after the discovery of some fragments of the notorious Piltdown Man. This was regarded as possibly the 'missing link' by some of the scientific community. However, after considerable examination, this was completely ruled out.

During the First World War, Teilhard served as a stretcher bearer in the medical corps. When he returned home after the war, he taught at a Catholic university for some time. Then he went off to China, to help set up a Catholic mission there. While he was in the Far East, he wrote what is regarded as his best and most engaging work, *The Phenomenon of Man*, between 1938 and 1940. Unfortunately, his superiors barred him from publishing his writings because of what they regarded as a pantheistic strain in his work. Most of what Teilhard wrote had to wait until after his death before it was published.

Teilhard came home to France from time to time, usually for short periods, but he finally settled in the US, where he died in 1955. While he was in America, he continued to write such books as *The Mystic Millennium, The Spiritual Power of Matter* and *The Growth of One Mind.*

However, it was the earliest book, *The Phenomenon of Man*, which is best remembered today. In that work, he looks at the span of human history, from its beginnings in the primeval past right through to the Unity of the Species and beyond, to our eventual extinction in the distant future. He deals with the facts in the broadest possible terms.

In the course of his work, he comes up with some intriguing suggestions. One of the most significant is the concept of the noosphere, which he claimed is a new layer of consciousness, which is circling the globe. It has been suggested that this is a prediction of the internet, almost fifty years before it was invented.

In his writings, he suggests that the whole universe is bound together, so that we are moving towards an inner connectivity and unity, which he calls the Omega Point.

The Phenomenon of Man was very favourably reviewed when it first came out in the middle of the last century, but Teilhard's reputation dipped during the following decades. However, it has risen significantly in recent years, and many of his ideas are being looked at and questioned again.

He is seen and recognised as a dedicated evolutionist, who worked to bring about a new and more positive relationship between science and religion, between the material and spiritual, the position of evolution as a positive force and to explore the ambiguous relationship between man and machines.

Today, de Chardin has many active and vocal admirers around the globe, and there are a number of societies dedicated to exploring his pioneering ideas, suggestions and prophesies.

Colin Wilson

Colin Wilson was a wide-ranging and versatile writer who produced seventy books on a variety of subjects, such as crime, sexual deviance, biography, music, drink, the occult, philosophy and mysticism. Despite his many and varied interests, he claimed that in his working life, he only had one abiding interest. This was his continuing search for the evolutionary path that would take him to a higher level of consciousness and development.

Colin was born in Leicester, England in 1931. He left school at sixteen to work in a variety of jobs. He spent time as a teaching assistant, as a labourer in a plastic factory and as a cleaner in a coffee shop, before he wrote his first book, a sociological study called *The Outsider*, at twenty-four. This was an engrossing study, which looked at the lives and work of important writers and thinkers like Kafka, Barbusse, Camus, Hemingway, Hesse, Sartre, Wells and Laurence, who all felt alienated from their communities. Wilson tried to define and understand the nature of their alienation.

The book was very well received, with some outstanding critical reviews and it became a controversial best seller. Wilson never achieved the acclaim or sales with his subsequent books, but there certainly was an intriguing and evolutionary trajectory with the work that followed.

His second book *Religion and the Rebel* looked at the spiritual and material influence that religion played on a number of prominent individuals but he decided that, although many of the questions dealt with the meaning of life and spiritual values, the answers provided did not meet the needs of the day. He then turned from religion to Existentialism in a number of subsequent books but he had to admit that in an age of defeat, despair and pessimism, making up your life as you went along and reinventing yourself are not the answer to the question of meaning, to his satisfaction.

He looked briefly at sex, crime and drink, and although he had some nice things to say about masturbation and tantric sex, one gathers that he was not overly impressed. He went on to consider the occult and wrote a number of books on the subject well. Then he tried his hand at science fiction, possibly impressed by H.G. Wells, but he remained dissatisfied.

He finally came to the life and work of Andrew Maslow, an American psychoanalyst. Wilson was particularly taken by

Maslow's 'Hierarchy of Needs', especially his concept of 'The Peak Experience', which was at the top of the hierarchy-of-needs pyramid.

Wilson came to believe that the Peak Experience (PE) could transform our everyday way of life and allow us to rise to a higher level of consciousness and development. Unlike Maslow, who claimed that PE could only come to us unannounced and unbidden, and disappeared after a short spell, Wilson believed that PE could be called up and retained, taking us to a whole new level. He devoted his last book, *Super Consciousness*, to the subject and went on to claim that this work could be used as a handbook for achieving PE as an exalted state of well being, positivity and creativity. He went on to show how the process worked for him.

Curiously enough, I felt that Wilson was closer to the beginning of his exceptional long journey, than the end. I was disappointed that he did not get a chance to tell us more before he died.

Wilson believed that most of us live at a level of everyday reality, and that this is not the best we can achieve or expect. He was certain that we could achieve much more and improve a great deal more by following our ability, by using our imagination, intelligence and creative powers in certain ways. It was unfortunate that he was taken before he could provide us with more evidence in a structured way but he does point out the direction, which he feels we should go. Hopefully, others will take up the challenge in the future.

It seems a real pity that he did not feel he could work with others in a dedicated group, to find collective answers to some of the evolutionary questions he posed. Unfortunately, he insisted on working alone. However, I feel that Wilson made a useful and valuable contribution to the debate on evolution, by highlighting the importance of consciousness and the way we think and feel that evolution will take us in the foreseeable future.

Richard Dawkins

Richard Dawkins is best known as a writer and as an effective advocate of Darwin's evolutionary ides. He was born on 26 March 1941 in South Africa. He was brought up in England from early childhood and was a devout Anglican into his mid teens. Then he came into contact with Darwin's theories, which fired his imagination and changed his beliefs. He became an ardent follower of Darwin and has remained so ever since.

He trained at Oxford, where he became a professor of Zoology. Then he spent several years teaching at Berkeley in the USA. Eventually, he gave up teaching and since then, has devoted his time to writing, broadcasting and making documentaries. He is a gifted populariser with a very polished touch, which shows in books like *The Selfish Gene* and *The God Delusion*. He is a keen devotee of scientific atheism and seems to enjoy a good argument. Politically to the left, he has joined anti-war demonstrations and has called for legal rights to be granted to great apes.

His first book, *The Selfish Gene*, was published in 1976. It was a considerable success, and he has since written several works about his favourite topics, evolution and religion.

In the first chapter of *The Selfish Gene,* Dawkins has a number of interesting things to say about the behaviour of genes and their relationship with biological evolution. Later in the book, he introduces us to his own particular concept of 'memes', which is his most striking contribution to the evolutionary debate. The word now has wide circulation and in 1988, it was considered for inclusion in the *Oxford English Dictionary*.

He claims that memes are cultural objects: like books, computers or crucifixes. He goes further to suggest that the meme can replicate when it is in the process of transmission. Then it can evolve and develop a life of its own. As he sees it, the meme has a special relationship with the gene through memory or imitation.

As I understand it, Dawkins believes that evolution occurs not only through biological entities themselves, but it also comes through cultural transmission. He gives some examples, noting that language evolves through non genetic means. He points out, for instance, that it can be found in tunes, ideas, catchphrases, clothes, fashions, ways of making pots and building arches. Personally, I can see evolution at work more obviously, in the development of cars, planes, phones and computers.

There are also the interesting ideas about super consciousness, and the idea that evolutionary development for us humans will basically come through our minds, imagination, willpower, focusing and meditation. It is even possible that we may be able to gauge, measure and change the development and direction of our consciousness, and allow us to play a proactive role in evolving to a higher consciousness. This may possibly happen, using the technology that we have available, as Teilhard de Chardin hinted at.

In a later book, *The God Delusion,* Dawkins attempted to define and set out an ethical code for atheists, or possibly secular evolutionists. He drew up some notes, taking some ideas from an atheist's website and some notions of his own, about enjoying a robust sex life and other matters. These ideas may be admirable, but they hardly form a basis for a coherent programme.

Like some other critics, I find Dawkins too strident when he is writing about religion, which at one point, he compares with smallpox and regrets that it has not been as easy to eradicate as that disease. For some reason, it seems that in his later books, like *Outgrowing God,* that his tone and language suggest an old fashioned, fundamentalist preacher, and one is inclined to wonder if Dawkins is trying to turn evolution into a new religion.

Surely he can see that science and religion are different disciplines, with their own standards and approaches and that in some circumstances, they could even be regarded as complementary disciplines, which could help each other or even work together.

The suggestion that religion and science will come together at some point in the future is not an idea that Dawkins would come to entertain at any price. However, he should realise that religion, like everything else, has never stopped changing, developing and even evolving in strange and surprising ways – as Christianity came out of Judaism and later, how Islam was born out of the earlier faiths.

I believe that Dawkins's contributions to the evolutionary debate, and the one between science and religion has been stimulating to say the least. Dawkins's ideas about memes have been useful in widening the discussion, and may possibly be of lasting value, or may lead to something greater as we approach the Unity.

Greta Thunberg

The Green activist and schoolgirl campaigner, Greta Thunberg was born in Stockholm, Sweden in 2003. She first heard of Climate Change in 2011, when she was eight years old. She simply could not understand why so little was being done about it.

The situation worried her, making her feel sick and depressed. For a time, she stopped talking and eating, with the result that she lost two kilograms in a number of months. Her parents were naturally worried and brought her to see a doctor. She was eventually diagnosed as suffering from Asperger's Syndrome.

For two years, she complained, pleaded and argued with her parents, and eventually managed to get them to lower the family's carbon footprint. When this happened, she was encouraged by her parents' response, and felt that she might actually be able to make a difference.

In 2018, she won a prize in a writing competition, with a letter about the need for environmental change, in a local newspaper. When this was published, a reporter from Fossil Free Dalsland contacted her. He suggested some ideas, which would help to attract attention to the Climate Change crisis. Greta was taken by one of his ideas – a school strike. So, she decided to do something about it. She tried to get some of her school friends to join in, but none of them were interested. However, this did not stop her, and she determined to go ahead alone. When she told her parents what she intended to do, they were not at all impressed. They told her that if she went ahead with her plan, that they would not support her, and they asked her to forget the plan.

None of the negative criticism deterred her. On 20 August 2018, she sat in front of the Swedish parliament building where she handed out leaflets. The leaflets had a long list of facts about Climate Change, and the horrors we should expect in the near future. One of the first things that Greta did when she returned home was to put a note on Twitter and Facebook. A reporter saw a post on social media, wrote up an article in the local paper, and the newspapers began to take an interest in the campaign and the campaigner. A Swedish businessman called Ingmar Rentzhog was amongst those to notice and respond. He came to see her and to take pictures, which he publicised.

Some other students engaged in similar protests in their own cities and communities. Together, they organised a school Climate Strike movement, which they advertised as 'Fridays for the Future' and for some time, student strikes were held in Sweden and beyond. In a relatively short time, Greta's actions started a global movement against Climate Change, inspiring millions of young people to go on strike for our planetary welfare and for the future. Greta won a prestigious Prix Liberté as well as a Nobel Prize nomination.

In time, she came to regard her Asperger's not as a handicap but as a positive gift, as it enabled her to see the crisis in black and white terms.

Today Greta is known for her strong feelings and unyielding passion, for speaking out against public and political leaders, for their failure to take hard or significant action with regard to Climate Action. Since her strike movement, she has addressed heads of state at the UN, met with the Pope and has taken an American president to task for his inaction and dismissive approach to the crisis that will be with us soon. She is widely admired and criticised for her actions and her behaviour. Some people regard her as a foolish, uncontrollable brat and as a noisy exhibitionist, but the writer Margaret Attwood has suggested that she is like a modern Joan of Arc. It is really a pity that so many of the young are still unwilling to raise their heads above the parapet and tell us what they really think of these crises and our reaction to them.

Thunberg has no magic answers, though she is recommending that we take action together, while we can still do so, and while we still have some chance of making a difference. At a Climate Change march in 2018, she told listeners that if people were clearly aware of the absolutely hideous scenarios we will face, if we do not manage to keep global warming below 2 degrees centigrade, they would not need to ask why she was taking these actions and was doing all that she possibly could to warn us about what will be coming our way soon.

In 2019, Thunberg sailed across the Atlantic, from Plymouth in Southwest England to New York, on an 18-metre racing yacht, where she spoke at a packed meeting of the UN General Assembly. She suggested that what was happening was foolishly wrong. She said that she should be back at school in Sweden but she knew that people were definitely searching for hope. She asked the Assembly why they dared to act in the way they were doing. We were facing mass extinction but all the big countries wanted to talk about was economic growth. People were suffering and dying with the ecosystem collapsing, but what were we actually doing? Then she finished with a simple rhetorical question, 'Just tell me how we can carry on like this?'

I must admit that I am sorry that Greta Thunberg is the only female on my list of evolutionists. We certainly need more eloquent women who are willing to write or campaign about the problems we face in the future and are prepared to ask awkward questions.

Greta certainly deserves to be here, in the company of her peers. She started off with a single, hand-painted sign and moved on to get millions of young people to embrace the cause. She has shown us what one young person can do, and no doubt there will be others as we move forward with the evolutionary shift towards the Unity. If they do, they could certainly save us from so much of the trouble and danger ahead.

Tim Smit

Tim Smit was born in Scheveningen, the Netherlands in 1954. He grew up in England, where he graduated from Durham University. He was employed as a country archaeologist before he changed to spend 10 years in the record industry. Then he grew tired of the lifestyle and moved his family to Cornwall in 1987.

He teamed up with a local builder to restore a dilapidated old estate, which had been apparently forgotten. The estate had a marvellous walled garden, which Smit greatly enjoyed working in, helping to restore it to its former glory. When he finished working in the estate, Smit wrote a bestselling book called *The*

Lost Gardens of Heligan, about the rescue and renovation of the lost wonderland.

Looking around for a further venture, Smit was prompted to take on an even more ambitious project in an old mining quarry just outside St Austell, Cornwall. In 2001, he managed to complete the Eden Project, which has become one of the most popular attractions in Britain after Stonehenge, which is situated close by.

I must say, I was extremely impressed when I went down to visit the Eden Project five years after it opened. After wandering around, it seemed that the project combined and fused elements of the past, present and future. There were splendid botanical gardens with echoes of the nineteenth century, a marvellous theme park with echoes of the present and a compact, experimented scientific station, which seemed to be looking to the future. These elements seemed to have been brought together in a splendidly cohesive manner. In a strange and extraordinary way, this was like a glimpse into the future. This vision came to me as I looked down from the visitors' platform into the quarry, which was dominated by a couple of huge, plastic bubbles or 'Biomes' as they are called. These are the largest conservatories in the world, or so I have been told.

I found that the first Biome was packed with hundreds of plants, trees and creepers from the humid, tropical rainforests. While the second Biome houses flora and fauna from the Mediterranean, with a number of sights, sounds and displays from Africa and South America. To the right of the second dome, there is a smaller wooden structure called the 'core', which acts as an educational and experimental centre. While to the left of the first Biome, there is a fine outdoor stage, where musical shows are frequently performed in the good weather. Behind this and stretching up towards the exit, are a cluster of outdoor gardens.

Tim Smit says that the purpose of the Eden Project is primarily to bring together as many of the plants we depend on for our survival into one place. They have been set out in a way that is educational and entertaining at the same time. Smit now travels the world, spreading his positive and iconic eco-vision of how we can protect and preserve our species and the natural world from destruction and extinction, if we will only listen to the warnings, shift out of our comfort zones and take the necessary decisive action.

Smit believes that national populists and right-wing movements are symptomatic of the dying days of the old world, which will be replaced by global citizenship and spiritual regeneration. He would very much like to inspire and provoke people to disrupt the status quo, and shift us away from the grey zone, which he believes that universities and environmental organisations are morphing into. He says that it is time for us to understand where we must move to in the future. He feels that we should do our best to get back to a time when there was a wider exploration of ideas. This happened when scientists were natural philosophers, who worked closely with artists and engineers to invent the future.

As well as travelling as far as possible to spread his message, Smit is leading a team to develop a series of Eden-like projects, in Australia, New Zealand, the US and China. One of the projects, with a theme of ecological restoration, is planned for the historic city of Yan'an in northern China. While another of his experiments is an educational and training programme for adults and children, which is at the planning stage at the Sheng Lu vineyard at Beijing.

Closer to home, Smit is busy devising and planning an Eden Project for Northern Ireland on the banks of the River Foyle, near Derry City. This project will be based round an old stately home, in a local housing estate at Brooks Hall. The plan involves the restoration of a historic landscape, and it intends to develop a number of walled gardens for housing and display.

According to Smit, the key to successfully engaging people with their environment is to go to where people actually are, not to where we think they should be (as the Chinese Cultural Revolution showed). Then you show that it is cool and acceptable to be where people are.

I think that Smit has taken on board the old adage, about showing rather than telling. If we can possibly show different aspects of tomorrow's world, even if its only a glimpse of what is to come, then we could possibly introduce people to what seems impossible.

It is very important, if not essential, that we become consciously aware of what we could do and are capable of achieving. If we can do this in a way that is engaging and educational, so much the better. If it pays its way, as the Eden Project does, that is better still.

These are some of the lessons we can learn from Smit. He has also been able to link the past, the present and the future together in a cohesive way. All this is worthwhile and of value to us on our evolutionary journey to the Unity.

Yuval Harari

The historian and best-selling writer, Yuval Harari was born on 24 February 1976 in Kiryat Ata, Israel. He was a clever and intelligent boy who was happy enough to start school at six and skipped up a class the following year. At the age of nine, he was sent to a special school on Mount Carmel, where he felt uncomfortable as he was put under constant pressure to excel. He later claimed that most of what he knew came down to him from his wise, Polish grandmother.

He grew up a gloomy, moody and depressed teenager, who felt that the world around him made little sense. He did not find that his Jewish religion and background helped him at all. He went around asking his parents, teachers and anybody who would listen what life was all about and how he could best live in the world, as it seemed to be that most of those whom he asked did not know or care, and more or less ignored his concerns.

He read a great deal and seemed to take refuge in the past. He studied at the Hebrew University of Jerusalem and then moved to England, where he got a PHD at Oxford. He specialised in Medieval History and went on to teach it there.

It was when he was asked to give what he considered an academically unimaginative course on the Evolution of Human Thought that the idea off writing his first book, *Sapiens*, came to him and he started making notes. He began working on the book a little later, when he was teaching a course on World History. Gradually, the twenty lectures that he was delivering became the twenty chapters of *Sapiens*, which he subtitled, *A Brief History of Humankind*. He did not have much trouble in finding a publisher. The book sold extremely well at the start and became an international publishing sensation.

Yuval came out as a gay man when he was twenty-one, just as he was beginning to make sense of the world around him. At twenty-four, he began to practice meditation for two hours a day. He still goes on meditational retreats regularly. He finds that the practice clears his mind and helps him to focus on what he has to do.

Harari has written three books so far. The first, *Sapiens*, tells the story of the evolutionary revolutions that have shaped human history. He believes that it started with the cognitive development that kickstarted human history seventy thousand years ago. Since then, our awareness and empathy developed. We have experienced a number of remarkable revolutions in different areas, notably in agriculture and industry, which have helped our civilisations evolve in many surprising ways. Harari believes that we are still changing, developing and evolving in many different ways. He further sees us breaking the laws of natural selection, to replace them with those of intelligent design, and truly earn our designation of *Sapiens* as a species.

Harari's next book, *Homo Deus,* moves on to speculate the way he thinks that mankind is moving as a species. He explores the projects, dreams and nightmares, which he thinks will shape our immediate future in the present century. These range from our coming death to the creation of new artificial life forms, and the emergence of a new species, Homo Deus. This book asks fundamental questions about the future, about what it will bring and what we need to watch out for.

After considering the past and the future, his third work, which is called, *Twenty-One Questions for the Twenty-First Century,* has been described as "a brief history of the present". The questions here are mainly those that Harari has been asked during his lectures about the present day. He believes that we are more interested in terrorism, nationalism and migration than the problems that are more relevant for our own survival as a species. Here he is writing about Climate Change, technological disruption, artificial intelligence and bioengineering, which he sees as the really important questions on the horizon. He believes that in the chaotic, fast-moving world we live in, that he can offer some clarity and an interesting perspective, as a historian. I find that many of the things he has to say are apt, wide ranging, surprising and reasonably sane.

In his *Twenty-One Questions,* he looks at a variety of subjects, like the question of what will happen to the 'useless class' who have no work and no prospects. He asks whether those who gather information on us and use the data are, in fact, spying on us and collecting data for large, commercial organisations or governments. Not only this, but he looks at problems associated with nationalism, war and terrorism, Jewish physics, Christian biology and the value of meditation.

In recent times Harari has been lecturing, writing a book for children, and talking on YouTube. He suggests that the best way of dealing with our big problems on an international scale would be to tackle them on a global level. However, he is not suggesting some form of World Government, as he feels that kind of consideration is a long way off. However, he suggests that we need to think about and consider global community, which will be prepared to take decisive action when required. He believes that we have already got a global ecology and a global science, but we are still stuck with nationalist politicians.

To be quite honest, I cannot understand why he would not consider a World Government, or even a Global Federation, to prepare the world for the New World Order that is coming. It will be interesting to see what he has to say about them in his future work.

Harari is certainly an engaging writer and easy to read. He has looked at where we have come from, where we are now and where we are likely to go in the future. This makes you wonder what he will tackle next.

James Lovelock

The English biologist and inventor, James Lovelock was born on 26 July 1919 in Letchworth, Hertfordshire. He was educated at Manchester University where he studied chemistry. He began his career experimenting with and dissecting rats. He invented a sensitive instrument for the analysis of extra-terrestrial atmospheres. He is also credited with the invention of an electron captive detector.

The first formulation of his famous Gaia theory was in the 1960s. He claimed that it resulted from his work with NASA, which was concerned with detecting life on Mars. He came to believe that all living and non-living entities on Earth are part of an interlinking system that should be considered as a single organism, which he decided to call Gaia. This is the name of a Greek goddess, which was suggested to him by the British novelist, William Golding, who had written a modern classic novel called *Lord of the Flies.* In Greek mythology, Gaia is seen as a Mother Earth figure, who was regarded as the mother of the pantheon of the Gods.

After giving the matter considerable thought, Lovelock wrote about his ideas and speculations in a book simply called *Gaia,* which had a subtitle *A New Look at Life on Earth.* In this work, he suggested that the Earth was a living entity. He claimed that all of its parts, from the core of molten lava to its plants, animals and human beings, are all part of a single organism. Just as we are made up of cells, molecules and atoms, we can all be considered as a small but important part of a global entity. Lovelock goes on to suggest that the Earth can be viewed as a self-regulating organism, which is always striving to maintain its balance. He sees this in the same way that the human body maintains a relationship with its ever-changing external environment. Lovelock sees this as a purely scientific matter of checks and balances.

No doubt, it is possible to take this hypothesis a step further, by considering if it is possible that we are actually the nervous system of the Earth itself. Is it even possible that the globe itself, like the human race, is actually becoming more conscious and self aware. A number of ancient belief systems and theories have suggested that humans are part of a universal consciousness. More recently, Teilhard de Chardin suggested something along the lines in *The Phenomenon of Man.* It is interesting to consider that we are all part of an awakening globe, even possibly the brain, then we are part of the world itself, just as the waves are part of the ocean, and our brains are part of us, but cannot be regarded as the whole self.

At one point, Lovelock warned that if we only think of nothing but ourselves, of human greed and selfishness and ignore the natural health of the globe itself, that we are preparing ourselves for our destruction. Do we not have to give the Earth more consideration, respect and protection? She has taken care of us from the very beginning, provided us with food and shelter, heat and water and unlimited opportunities to realise our potential. However, if you look around us today and consider how we have depleted our resources and covered her with so much pollution, is it any wonder that we have a Climate Crisis on our hands? No wonder that some people have begun to ask, when will we stop to consider what we have done and even at this late stage, continue to do, despite the evidence?

Lovelock's concerns have been widely accepted and acknowledged by many in the scientific community. I feel that his ideas about Gaia are well worth exploring and considering in the debate about evolution, though it must be admitted that he has produced little hard evidence to show that Gaia is more than a theory. Like de Chardin however, he has certainly added an unusual personal dimension to the evolutionary debate. After all, where exactly would we be without the world around us?

Jacque Fresco

The American inventor and futurist, Jacque Fresco was born in Manhattan, New York on 16 March 1916, where he grew up in a traditional, middle-class, Jewish household. As a young man he was disturbed by the poverty he saw around him, caused by the Great Depression. In his late teens, he went hitch-hiking around the country, taking work wherever he could find it. He finally settled and worked as a technician until he was drafted in

1942. He spent most of the war years working and gaining experience as a technical engineer.

After the war, he went on to design low-cost housing in Los Angeles and later, he opened a small business as a psychological consultant. However, it was only when he brought a twenty-five-acre site at Venus, Florida in the 1980s that he began to realise his dreams. He found a partner and work mate in Roxanne Meadows, who helped him to work on his long-term 'Venus Project'. It is for this futuristic project that Fresco is remembered today.

In the last thirty years of his life, Fresco spent his time designing and planning, making videos of his ideal city and its environs. A number of these videos are still available on YouTube today. In them, he comes up with some intriguing ideas about our future in his 'Circular Cities' and a 'Resource-Based Economy'.

Fresco believed that we have sufficient resources available in the world today to meet all our needs and requirements as a species. As he saw it, the resources we have are not at all fairly distributed. According to reports, over three billion people cannot afford a healthy diet. As he sees it, this is one of the big challenges we face in an increasingly interdependent world, and the crazy inequality that we see around us.

Just consider that half of the world's population live on about €2 per day, while over one billion manage on just half of this. This is at the end of the spectrum, while on the other, one per cent own and control 20% of the world's wealth and resources. Fresco was appalled by the situation and went on to suggest that we should work to change this, and possibly even do without money at all. He said that our economies should be there to serve the 'need not greed' of the community. Everyone should be given enough to meet their basic needs and when they require anything else, we should be able to go to a Resource Centre, where we can borrow and use whatever is required from bed linen, cameras, clothes, fridges and televisions, just as we do with books from a library. We could return these items when we no longer need them. He also believed that we should have sophisticated machines and computers in public companies to produce whatever is required, and that this would leave us free to follow the vocations of our choice.

The main difficulty, as I see it, would be to find enough people to buy into Fresco's moneyless system. As far as I know, no resource-based economy has been tried or set up on a large scale in this part of the world. However, there have been some commune-based communities, like the Bruderhof (The Society of Brothers), where the pooling of resources was tried, while politically defensive communities were set up in Israel, shortly after the foundation of the state. Communes on a larger scale were attempted in Russia and China with very mixed results. We hear very little about communes since, and practically nothing about the abolition of money. There will be further attempts to reform, if not abolish the system in the next eighty years.

Fresco's other big idea, the circular city, certainly looks futuristic from the models that I have seen on YouTube. We find star-shaped buildings at the centre of his city designs. These are surrounded by widening rings of concentric hubs. The administrative and energy centres are housed in the star-shaped buildings. Beyond these, we have the business and factory hubs, while further out we have housing, apartments and other residential quarters. Still further out, we have covered and outdoor agricultural parks and sports arenas. Each of the circular hubs will be built with prefabricated concrete, slotted together. Fresco believed that our cities and towns grew and developed in too haphazard a fashion. He believed that the new cities would be more structured and cohesive affairs, planned and designed to meet the requirements of the 21st century.

So far, we have had no serious effort to build as he suggested, or to work on his sea cities, which will have to be built on stilts. While his aims are admirable and very possibly could make life easier for us, Fresco found great difficulty in raising money to build his prototypes to complete his projects and turn his dreams into realities.

Fresco has nearly always been regarded as too utopian a thinker to be taken seriously. At one point, he was asked why he thought that he had so much trouble realising his projects. His answer was simple – "Because I don't get on well with other people."

He may not have been able to realise his dreams of making the 'future by design' but his pioneering spirit, evolutionary zeal and willingness to think outside the box, hopefully, will inspire others to think and dream his future by design later in this century.

Tim Berners-Lee

The scientist and inventor, Tim Berners-Lee who created the World Wide Web was born in London, England in 1955. His parents worked as computer programmers for Ferranti and encouraged him to take an interest in computers from an early age.

Berners-Lee went to Oxford University in 1973, where he studied physics. While he was still at college, he actually managed to build a home-made computer using an old television set, a processor and some logic gates. Oddly enough, this computer worked surprisingly well and encouraged him to explore further when he graduated from college.

He was employed, for a time, as a software engineer before he left England to work for CERN in Switzerland. This is Europe's largest nuclear laboratory, and it is the home of the Large Hadron Collider, which is famous for its work in splitting atoms.

Shortly after he started at CERN, he recalled reading a book, which had captured his imagination when he was very young. This book was called *Enquire Within Upon Everything*. It struck him that the computers he was working with at CERN had the potential to be used as an electric version of the book. He felt that the communication demands of the laboratory could basically transform the way the world communicates, if handled properly. It prompted him to write a computer programme called simply 'Enquire'. This initially aimed to connect academics with the projects at CERN. This programme showed how to store information and track the connection between people and projects in the different parts of CERN. From an early stage, he claimed that there was a possibility that the system could be used outside the CERN setting, to communicate on a wider and much larger scale, and could possibly even be accessed and used by anyone with a computer.

He called this the World Wide Web and, in fact, it was the precursor to the internet as we know it. In the beginning, it was sponsored and used by the academics at CERN and the US government, who found a use for it as a military tool. Berners-Lee became convinced, at this point, that it could definitely become a tool for universal communication. In 1981, he published a manifesto, which offered detailed instructions for programmers and showed how you could build your own website. Berners-Lee urged and finally persuaded CERN to launch the World Wide Web for free, by putting it into the public domain instead of patenting it. This is just what has happened, and Berners-Lee has remained true to his ideals. He could possibly have become a billionaire if he had patented it, but he wanted to ensure the Web would be used in the widest possible way, for the benefit of mankind.

Writing about the Web in in 2008, he suggested that its essential purpose was not to connect machines but to bring people together, and that is what it has done. Today, the internet has developed in an extraordinary way and at present, it has the largest multimedia-based library in the world (Wikipedia), which is consulted by millions all over the globe every day. The Web has become the Mecca for online shoppers (Amazon), and the personal communications tool for anybody with a computer (Facebook and Twitter).

From the internet's earliest days, Berners-Lee has been a constant advocate for a fair and democratic social system, worldwide in its reach, bringing political, social and economic benefits to everyone on this planet. The internet even helped two US presidents (Obama and Trump) to raise money for their elections and stay close to their political bases.

Berners-Lee claimed that he may have invented the Web but that all of us have made it what it is today. The most intriguing aspect and feature of the internet is that it is the beginning of a process that is growing, developing and evolving every day before our eyes, in the most surprising ways. We are like children playing around with a marvellous new machine, not yet fully aware of what it can do or achieve for us in tomorrow's world.

Section Four

~ Glimpsing the Future ~

Chapter Twelve

Glimpsing the Future

In the last chapter, we looked at a number of those whom I consider played an important part in the debate on evolution. As I have already noted, Darwin played an important part in bringing about significant change by reflecting, speculating and considering where we have come from, while the evolutionists who followed after him used his ideas, read the signs and speculated on where we are going in the future.

I have to admit that I find it more intriguing and engaging to look forward than back. So, in this section, I will look over a number of different aspects of the foreseeable future, as I see them, coming up. They are only glimpses, but I would like to consider how we can move forward from our present positions, and suggest what we can do with, or use them if we possibly can. Of course, I would not be too surprised if we do not see a number of the ideas manage to surface or work out as I suggest. However, I have no doubt that a number will. If they do, they should help to make this a better world, for ourselves and for our children.

As Plato put it, "The best way to predict the future, is to invent it."

What I would like to offer here, are a few ideas or glimpses into the future. They could come true, but only if we want them to, and are prepared to work for them.

I believe that the period we are entering is one in which we will see tremendous change, in so many aspects of our lives. Some of these will be brought about by the problems and crises we will face, and some will come through the choices we make. No doubt, some of the decisions we decide to take will be wrong or even disastrous, but others will be life-enhancing and inspiring. Hopefully, we will have learned from the disasters and mistakes of the past, and we will be able to use our intelligence, imagination, wealth and creativity as we move forward towards the Unity and discover our potential.

Chapter Thirteen

Approaching the Unity

Our basic survival as a species depends on how we cooperate and live with others. When you look and think about our long-term growth and development in the past, you will see that we have moved from being hunter-gatherers, through a number of phases, in agriculture, religion, science, industry and technology. At each stage we needed to find new ways of living and working together. Each move forward has depended on finding a new and different way of cooperating as individuals and as a community.

Over a considerable period, we have managed to bring together a loose, not very efficient world community, with three desirable levels. These three levels are the underdeveloped, the developing and the developed states, who just about tolerate each other. This is by no means a desirable arrangement and there are very few who believe that its parts work well together. However, it is a reality and possibly looks well and quite impressive from a distance. Nevertheless, when you look closer, you can see the signs of strain, difficulty and crisis.

Considering this, I believe that we have reached a decisive point in our development because of our numbers and our awareness of what is happening. This will bring the numerous races, tribes and communities who live on this planet together as one people, in a new and intriguing way. This will enable us to work in a new and more effective way, which is a more sane, sensible and appropriate way. We will take a brave and evolutionary move, resolve our differences, tear down the barriers that result from prejudices and keep us apart. We will even come to accept that the world is one country.

If we decide to change, prepare for the crises ahead of us and move forward to deal with them. We will need to alter the way that we live now. This will give us the opportunity to transform the world, make it a more secure place to live in, and prepare us for the Unity, which is fast coming toward us.

As individuals, there are a number of ways in which we will need to change. First of all, we will need to change the way we think. We must be open to see the world in a better way. We have been given an opportunity and the power to radically alter the world in a much more positive way. We need to learn how to do things together cooperatively, working with strangers, foreigners and those whom we do not particularly like, rather than fighting, competing and thinking of 'number one' as the best and only possible option that is available or worth considering.

We will need to consider how we work, how we see each other, and realise that their needs are as wide as our own. As a good doctor said during the recent pandemic, "We are all in this together."

We need to understand and realise that we will achieve a good deal more when we are working together, than when we are alone. There are lessons that we can learn from other species, like ants, birds and bees. It is necessary for us to learn from others, wherever and whenever we can, and that this can be done negatively or positively. It is not simply a question of waiting for emergencies. We need to change the way we treat and use our resources, like food and durables of all kinds. We need to recycle it, instead of throwing away and dumping so much. When Resource Archives are up and running, information will be available.

We need to be more questioning about our goals and beliefs and be prepared to change them when necessary. We need to know if there are better ways of doing things and be prepared to change if we think others are doing things in a better way. For instance, we should be prepared to help and serve on the voluntary corps and do community service when it is required.

The above are just a few of the ways that we will need to change. At present, many of us would consider them to be obvious, unnecessary, impractical or even undesirable. Times and attitudes will change, the goalposts will be moved and the future may be a strange and a different place from what we imagined it will be from our present perspective. No doubt, we will make many changes for the common good. The time will come when we need to speak out as whistle blowers. When we believe that something is wrong or grossly unfair, we need to say so.

Socially, we should not expect to see too many changes in a positive direction until after the half-century. We have a couple of crises brewing on the horizon. In the coming decades, we will see the ravages of Climate Change. Hopefully, it will be not nearly as devastating as predicted if we are ready and prepared for it.

Then, within a decade or so, we will have the devastation caused by the Last Great War. We already have had a glimpse of what this will bring, with the images on the television of the war in Ukraine, which almost looks like a throwback to the blitz in London during the Second World War. Hopefully, the Last Great War will be an end to our teenage years.

In the mid years of the present century, we will begin to see real change as we move from the chaos, with the inauguration of the Global Federation, which will gradually replace the dysfunctional United Nations. Initially, this new organisation will not take over from the United Nations. It will work beside the older organisation, helping and assisting, dealing with the different crises as they come up, and it will gradually take over its duties and responsibilities. However, its main duty will be to prepare the globe for the World Government, which will be in place by the end of the century.

The Global Federation will be a good deal more proactive than its predecessor. It would not have the Security Council to tie its hands, and it will have the experience of the UN to help it to negotiate our way through the problems that we have to face.

The Global Federation will do what it can to help the nation states to rebuild what is left of our battered civilisation. The process of change will be aided and encouraged by a great religious revival, which will come about shortly after the Global Federation takes charge. This religious revival will be spurred on by the new, global religion with an evolutionary base. It will have a new and appropriate social democratic agenda, be prepared to offer a strong set of ethical principles and an inspiring vision for the next century. The religion will work with science and technology to bring the material and the spiritual into a new alignment and working relationship. This will prepare the world for a new age, which will have its own particular problems, as well as opportunities and a very different way of looking at things. The big and important difference from today will be that we face the future together, as one people, working as a cohesive and cooperative whole, to take the next evolutionary step together, and aware that we are moving forward to realise our potential, which will be so much more than we ever imagined was possible, for ourselves as individuals and as a species.

Chapter Fourteen

The End of War

A number of eminent historians, notably Harari and Pinker, have suggested that we live in a relatively peaceful environment compared with our prehistoric ancestors. It seems that during the Stone Age, between ten and twenty per cent of those who lived in those troubled times, died of violence inflicted on them by their contemporaries, whereas in the last century, only between one and two per cent were killed in wars and violent exchanges. This may seem surprising when you consider that this figure includes all those who were killed in the two global conflicts that were fought in the last century. However, it is very likely that we will be faced with the Last Great War some time around the middle of this century, when the number of casualties will, in all probability be a great deal higher, than in the previous conflicts.

Hopefully, when we call a stop to the madness, we will be prepared to think of ways of preventing and bringing an end to all further wars, by the end of the century. Undoubtedly this may sound over optimistic and much too ambitious a target, but if we are prepared to focus and concentrate on the problem, in the same way that scientists and medics tackled diseases in the last century, wiping out leprosy, tuberculosis and smallpox so effectively, I have no doubt that we could combat, halt and eventually consign war, in its many forms, to the history books and the archives. In fact, it is one of the curiosities of the age that we have not even considered this as a possibility.

Even if we manage, by some strange miracle of fate, to avoid the catastrophe of a Third World War, millions will undoubtedly die in conflicts like Yugoslavia, Afghanistan and Ukraine, and other needless engagements. Individually, there is little we can do to stop wars happening, despite our best efforts but together, we can and will do just that if we are prepared to work hard enough together. We certainly would not be united if we do otherwise.

Just think for a moment – if we are prepared to stop butchering each other and agree to work together with a positive global agenda, we could make this an infinitely better place for most of us, even if there were a few dissenters who were determined to object. We would be able to look forward with hope, vision and expectation, and not back with a nostalgia for a past that never was.

There are a number of good reasons why we should finally leave war to the history buffs, to heavyweight novels like, *War and Peace* and to Hollywood blockbusters like *Gone with the Wind*.

(1) **Collateral Damage**: millions of innocent men, women and children suffered and died, in terror bombings, killing sprees and uncontrollable fires in the two world wars. These people were simply in the wrong places at the wrong times. Later, they were simply regarded as collateral damage of the murder machines. Today we can catch a glimpse of this madness, in the Russian invasion of Ukraine, with the bombing of hospitals and schools, civilians sleeping in cellars and huge movements of migrants from the horror zones. All this goes to show how easily we can slip back into the horrors of yesteryear. It could simply come with the flick of a switch.

(2) **Cannon Fodder**: hordes of energetic and enthusiastic young men died or were crippled in the most terrifying circumstances during the countless mad wars we fought right through the twentieth century. The saddest and craziest part of the story, and their individual parts, was

that so many of these boys and young men had only the haziest and sketchiest ideas of just why they were being sacrificed or drawn into prejudiced and pointless conflicts.

(3) **The Waste of Resources**: it seems extraordinary that we waste our resources of manpower and material in military operations of all kinds. We raise huge armies and stockpile enormous quantities of weapons to protect ourselves, our families and friends from potential aggressors and attacks. Though it must be admitted that some of us look around to see which of our neighbours we can argue or pick a fight with.

It seems so foolish when we could use our resources to feed and care for the hungry and deprived, look after the sick and the homeless and make this the best of all possible worlds.

(4) **Relearning Old Lessons**: when we consider the destruction and devastation caused by so many wars, fought in so many places, with so little to show for these mad engagements in the past one hundred and twenty years, one wonders how much longer it will be before we learn. What could have been achieved if we had come together in the early years of the last century, to create a better, more peaceful and wiser world, instead of trying to better each other by bickering, torturing each other over territory?

Every day since 'the war to end all wars', there have been wars, conflicts and disputes in different parts of our small globe. What do you think this says about us as a species, and how long can we possibly go on in this way?

When you look around the world, we live in, you can see that we have made notable progress on the technological and medical fronts. People are living longer and the general health of mankind is gradually improving. We have been remarkably slow in other respects, especially in the political and economic spheres. In so many ways, we have wasted time, energy and mind power, waged two hot, global conflicts and one cold one. Too often, we seem to take two steps back for every one that we take forward with our national, populist leaders.

(5) **Game Playing Exercises**: during the past hundred years or so, we have had civil wars in Spain, India, Yugoslavia and Ireland, with families and communities divided. Their wars were as vicious as those between strangers and went on until the participants felt that they had had enough. When this happened, both sides threw in their arms and went home. Later, the survivors had to pick up the pieces and make some kind of accommodation with each other, before they retired home, with little to show for their troubles, to the 'old normal', with only a change of flag or government to show for it.

(6) **The Beneficiaries**: usually a small minority benefits from war. There are some, like planners and arms dealers, politicians, military men and an assortment of gophers, usually on the winning side, who come out from these engagements with their tails wagging. The rest of us have to get down on our knees to clean up before we reshuffle our lives, tighten our economic belts and reorder our misguided beliefs.

For some reason, there is a widespread acceptance that war is simply a force of nature, and ultimately beyond our control. It is said that there have been wars, which crop up in expected and unexpected places, and that there will always be military engagements as long as we can find people willing to fight them.

Others believe that they are a kind of 'natural selection' and work themselves out with the 'survival of the fittest'. However, I am inclined to believe that wars are actually a demonstration of our immaturity as a species, which we will eventually grow out of in time. Do we actually believe that brawn is better than brain, or that it is always the last, best option of Homo Sapiens?

Unfortunately, in the past, the religions have usually found excuses for war and its many warriors. The Hindu avatar was a soldier, while Christians who had a pacifist leader, found an ingenious justification for war early on, in Saint Augustine's 'Just War' doctrine. The Jewish God figure often appears to be a vengeful and warlike old man, while Mohammed, the Islamic prophet, was a political and military leader.

As we approach our maturity, we must find ways to control ourselves and leave our more primitive tracts behind. I have no doubt that religion, in the future, will not approve or accommodate this kind of behaviour. If it does, it will have to produce some very good reasons or explanations for doing so.

While we still seem to be very slow learners, I have no doubt that we will come to realise that war, especially when it involves the massacre of millions of our fellow human beings, is one of the most abhorrent crimes in the book, and that we finally must call a stop to it in all its manifestations. I am aware that we cannot just stop it tomorrow or wish it away with prayers and a magic lamp, but we must wean ourselves off it in the foreseeable future. It is one of the most serious problems that we have to deal with, and it should be on the top of our agenda of the difficulties that we need to face.

At present, the European Union offers us an example of how we could tackle the problem, or at least make a start if we wanted to think about it. When the Global Federation phases it out towards the end of the century, it will certainly mark an important milestone as we move through the portals of the New World

Order, into another age, with a fresh agenda, without war in it. It cannot come too soon.

Chapter Fifteen

Art

Looking back to the start of the 20th century, it has been noted that there was a great deal of optimism about the future. People seemed to feel that the good times were coming our way, and that we should begin the new century in a new way with fresh expectations.

A number of the great and not-so-great artists of the time, especially amongst the painters and sculptors, were hoping to find fresh ways and opportunities to show how they felt and thought. They moved away from realistic representation and naturalism, on to impressionism, pointillism and expressionism, searching and experimenting with paint and other materials in all sorts of ways. Some artists like Kingsley, Mondrian and Malevich began to produce completely abstract works, which seemed to be a radical break with what had gone before, offering a new and different way of looking at the world, and starting afresh. Other artists like Cézanne, Picasso, Braque and Matisse remained a good deal closer to figuration but worked to use paint for their own purposes, often manipulating what they thought and observed in new and original ways.

Gradually many of their fellow artists came to follow their example, occasionally in groups and so, new movements appeared. The most prominent of these new movements were Cubism, which emphasised basic shapes; Futurism, which sought to depict the speed of change in the modern world; Orphism, which sought to experiment with colour shapes; Dada, which concentrated on how nonsense and absurdity could be used creatively and Surrealism, which explored the world of dreams and the subconscious. The ironic and often playful work of Marcel Duchamp suggested that whatever the artist described as art or signed as art was most definitely art. At one point, he exhibited an urinal and signed it as R. Mutt.

This takes us up to the Second World War, when some of the more important European artists emigrated to the US. They helped to establish New York as the main centre of Modern Art. In the post-war period, one of the first fully fledged art movements was established there. This was abstract work. This was followed by Pop Art, which drew its inspiration from contemporary advertising and comic books. It was during this period that really big money moved in to manipulate and hype up the market for Modern Art. This saw an inflation of prices, the use of contemporary art as status symbols and the emergence of superstars like Jackson Pollock and Andy Warhol as colourful performers. It has been suggested that much of the money came from conservative, political and business sources and even the CIA. It seems that they favoured unideological art that would blend, be acceptable and less threatening to the status quo.

Pop Art was followed by a quick succession of bland and inoffensive movements, which claimed to look at and examine different aspects of contemporary life. There was Op Art, which played optical games and looked at colour in engaging ways, Minimalism, which felt that the less said the better, Conceptualism and Land Art. Then we had Postmodernism, which took what it wanted from earlier styles and movements.

At this stage, galleries began to show photos and videos more widely. This certainly added more variety to the work on show, but much of it has little to say and less to offer. Still, some of this work took an interest in social issues and theories, like the effects of Climate Change, migrational surges, public protests, waste management, pandemics and the blossoming of graffiti art.

While modern artwork has certainly allowed artists to express themselves as individuals and groups, it has not said a great deal about the problems and crises we face (like world wars, nuclear devastation, the great depression, ideological conflicts) or offered us visions of a better life. We really need artists who can offer us insights, wisdom, visions or answers. In recent years, some of the evolutionists whom I mentioned earlier have attempted to ask difficult questions, offer us acceptable answers and some hope and vision, using art to do so. I am writing here about the likes of Jacque Fresco with his Florida-based Venus Project, Tim Smit with his Eden Project in Cornwall and Tim Berners-Lee with the World Wide Web, which has given us a new way to communicate. They are not artists in a traditional sense, but they have taken the advice given to performance artists, to show rather than to tell. No doubt, more artists will do this in the future, in many different and surprising ways.

Since Postmodernism, we have heard little about art movements. No doubt, we will see many artists doing their own thing in individual ways and no doubt, new movements like Digital Art will emerge, some of which will express a new globalist or evolutionary ethic in painting, sculpture and in other ways. I can see a need for a simple global symbol, to express a new global identity. I can already see huge, metal, stone and plastic sculptures, which will use circular global motifs, sited and built on the tallest hills and mountains of different countries and states, as they become part of the Global Federation. Each of these countries will take a different approach to this sculptural project. Some may even cut out or draw the symbol on the side of monuments but they will all be part of a collective movement to suggest Unity.

Artists and architects will design new global cities, and we will see alternative visions of the Eden Project appearing in different parts of the world, expressions of a new global unity, telling different stories, possibly with an eco-basis.

The future, in a sense, is an open book for us. Evolution offers us a wonderful opportunity to plan for a better world. Artists and evolutionists will work together to express that vision in exciting and marvellous ways, which will help take us to a new evolutionary level.

No doubt, the cinema will contribute to bringing the vision to life. During the past century, films have looked into the future and speculated on our evolutionary potential, often with inspiration from popular science fiction novels and short stories. We have explored AI, brainwashing, group and hive intelligence, miniaturisation, cloning, time travel, planetary and star travel, alien life forms, flying saucers and invisibility. This by no means exhausts the list. No doubt, films will continue to draw from science fiction novels and other sources, and just possibly deal with them in a serious and adult fashion.

The films may even encourage the younger generations to go where no man has ever gone before. They would hardly benefit the rest of us if the moguls and money men are allowed to drag us back to the past, to discover our future by repeating our pasts, to make themselves richer.

Chapter Sixteen

Basic Income

Why do so many people, living in rich and powerful, first-world countries, still have to live in poverty and deprivation in this day and age. It is unfortunate, to say the least, that so many men, women and even children die of starvation, homeless and living in shacks and tents, and are occasionally found rotting in ditches and laneways, while others enjoy the most fabulous lifestyles and live in luxury, sometimes in the same neighbourhoods. This seems extraordinary when you consider the resources that we have available, which could put an end to all this. However, as things stand, such poverty does not rate very highly on the agenda of the problems we face. This very possibly happens because the situation has been with us for so long, that most of us hardly notice it at all, or consider it someone else's business.

No doubt, we will get around to deal with this and other problems of a similar nature sometime in the middle-distance future. However, the question needs to be answered, why have we left it so long to deal with this kind of difficulty in a structured and methodical manner? We could deal with it now, without too much difficulty. Or should we admit that it is simply too much for us to even consider or look at? Or should we simply kick the problem down the road, and leave it to our children and their children to finally clear it up and keep the streets clean?

When the change does come, it will be slow and methodical. Only gradually will it speed up, and we will expect to see progress and results. There may be arguments and objections from those who want to protect their own income, interests, or feel that there are better ways of spending money than on the undeserving poor, but it will become clear and obvious eventually, that a fair and equitable system for all must help and benefit us all.

These problems and difficulties have been considered by philosophers and thinkers down through the ages. Over five hundred years ago, Thomas More, in his thoughtful and influential book, *Utopia* asked more or less the same question. This has been repeated by economists and social thinkers of all stripes since then right up to Friedrich Hayek and Milton Freeman, but there have been few really satisfactory answers, or practical solutions.

The main reason for this lies in the fact that it is seldom on the political agenda and this becomes clear when you read through the history books. There you will find that people living in times past lacked the resources and the mindset to deal with these problems. No doubt, many would have liked to do something to make matters better. Christianity, which many of them believed in wholeheartedly, certainly recommended the virtues of love, charity and empathy. However, the simple lifestyles of ordinary people did not change a great deal from decade to decade and even from century to century. In medieval times, it was widely believed that 'the poor will be always with us' and more harshly that, 'if you don't work, you don't eat'. In those days, it was left to the clergy and the gentry to look after the poor, the deprived and dispersed peasants when times were hard.

When the Industrial Revolution arrived, things began to improve but only gradually, as our social consciences developed. However, no great effort was made to introduce a social welfare system until the German Chancellor, Bismarck brought in the pension in the late 19th century. Workhouses opened in England and other European countries to deal with plague and poverty. In the Middle and Far East, it remained to kin and family to support and assist the older generation who could no longer work. In the 20th century, the ideas of human brotherhood and the possibility of a beautiful people who could take us to a new level was perverted by the social movements of Nazi Germany and Communist Russia and later, Red China. These regimes installed despots and tyrants, who simply made life miserable for their people, and often for the rest of us.

However, the idea and notion of a better world was simmering in the background, with the concept of social justice, the eradication of war as a form of diplomacy, a universal educational system and a world health organisation have been shifting slowly from dream to reality. We have the example of Britain's National Health System, which was set up shortly after the Second World War and has become one of the essential public organs of the British State.

Other social models like the World Court, the World Health Organisation and the United Nations themselves are far from perfect, but they give us some idea of where the world is heading, and what is needed in the foreseeable future.

Experiments in a Basic Income system are being worked on today, as they will help to lift the most deprived people out of absolute poverty, ensure that everyone has a basic level of support and gradually improve the living conditions of those in developing and undeveloped countries, bringing them up to the level of the developed nations. No doubt, this will take a considerable time before we see such a project work, but we need to start as soon as possible to get this project up and running.

Experiments in developing a Basic Income system have been in operation in a number of different countries for some time. Some of these schemes have been tied to welfare, while others have no restrictions at all. Different approaches have been used in Kenya, Namibia, Brazil, India, South Africa and Sweden. However, the most surprising and startling examples have been in America and Switzerland, two of the most prosperous and wealthy countries in the world today.

Just twenty years after the Second World War, while the US was fighting with North Vietnam and a large and vocal section of the younger generation was demonstrating for an end to foreign wars, a number of prominent economists, led by John Kenneth Galbraith, wrote to Congress suggesting that the country would not meet its responsibility to its citizens until everyone in the country was assured of an income no less than the economically realised definition of poverty. The following August, the then president, Richard Nixon sponsored a bill that would have provided a modest basic income for all of his fellow citizens. He called this the most marvellous piece of social legislation in his country's history. It may not have been quite that, but it was a much better deal than what existed there at the time.

The press and the polls were enthusiastic and very positive in their response, and the indications were that the provisions would pass without difficulty. However, the bill was rejected in the Senate. The following year, the bill was again rejected after a partisan debate. It finally died a death after its attempted revival several years later.

The Swiss held a referendum in 2016 on instituting a National Basic Income but unfortunately, the voters rejected the proposal. It seemed that the scheme was doomed to failure, and we will have to wait fifty years before it will be universally adopted and endorsed by the World Bank.

Just why these attempts to introduce such a progressive initiative failed for so long is difficult to understand or appreciate. It seemed more than just a good idea to help bring health and lift nations out of poverty. The idea undoubtedly upset the status quo. It was suggested that the scheme would be too expensive to introduce, that people would work less, if they received a guaranteed income and that the idea would be too divisive to implement. However, like the social welfare scheme and the British National Health System, when the basic income has been introduced and up and running for some time, it will be accepted as a necessary part of the social infrastructure.

Chapter Seventeen

Religion

The influential sociologist, Max Webber (1864-1920) suggested that religion would die out within a century, as we moved forward to increasingly use the scientific method and approach. I believe that he was a little presumptive when he suggested this, as religion has been one of the great game changers of history, together with power, politics and money. It still seems to be with us in many different shapes and forms, some of which appear to be thriving. Again and again, history has shown us that religion has a fantastic ability to reinvent itself in different ways. Like so much else, it has managed to evolve, change its shape and find a new way to meet the needs of the time.

We can see this at work in the great religions. For instance, Judaism moved on to morph into Christianity, taking with it many of the beliefs and traditions of the older faith, while it disregarded and changed others, and assumed a radical new form. Several hundred years later, Christianity was followed by Islam, which moved in another social direction.

We find the same kind of thing happening in the Far East, where one of the oldest of the great religions, Hinduism, found a radical new approach and Buddhism was born. The new religion spread out and developed in all sorts of ways, to be followed by Sikhism, which arrived in the 16th century. Oddly enough, all of these religions are still with us, with different social messages, but the same spiritual teaching, which has been called the 'golden mean'.

Despite their close relationship, many of the believers in the different religions fight, bicker and kill each other, even when they profess, more or less, the same creeds. We find Catholics and Protestants in Christianity and Sunni and Shia in Islam, arguing and fighting over different points and interpretations of their faith. One notes that the believers of the different faiths seem to be better at stressing their differences rather than their similarities and what they share in common. This is possibly the reason why there are so many subdivisions in Christianity and Hinduism, when you think about the hundreds of different belief systems in Christianity that have grown and developed from the simple story of a Jewish carpenter, who believed that he had come from God to deliver a simple message to mankind, of peace, love and empathy.

In his second book *Religion and the Rebel*, the English writer, Colin Wilson observed that we have many religious questions about 'the meaning of life' but few satisfying religious answers. Until recently, many of us were brought up in our parents' religion and adapted it to meet our spiritual needs but more often than not, ignored or disregarded its difficult points. I think that many of us find that religions have much to offer like, for instance, a comforting vision of the next life, peace of mind and hope for the future, with prayer and meditation, an ethical framework for a better life and a supportive attitude towards fellow believers. There is much here that the scientific approach has not been able to match. When the scientist and notable atheist, Richard Dawkins offered an ethical code for atheists in *The God Delusion*, he fell well short of what was required, and his formula seemed extremely weak.

While many of the religious systems today look back nostalgically to a golden age of saints, martyrs and miraculous happenings, some of the more recent variants come along with a scientific tag, like Christian Science and Scientology. There are a number of others with a strong evolutionary strain and an engaging vision of the future, though some are more plausible and believable than others.

One of the more engaging is Bahá'í, which, surprisingly, emerged from Shia Islam, during the second half of the 19th century. Its founder was an Iranian landowner called Mirza Husain Ali, who took the name Bahá'u'lláh (Glory of God). He claimed that the unity of the human race was imminent, as we have reached a decisive evolutionary tipping point in human history and will come together in a new, empathetic way as one people.

He was banished and imprisoned on Mount Carmel in Israel, where he remained for the rest of his life. He encouraged his followers to go out and spread his teachings, transcribed a number of books and laid the foundations for a world religion, which we call the Bahá'í Faith.

It has been growing gradually in the twentieth century and the first half of the twenty-first, preparing for the unification, with its worldwide network of local and national assemblies encouraging the formation of the Global Foundation and the election of a world government, which will be in place in the foreseeable future. It is one of the few social movements that is planning and organising for the New World Order, emphasising unity and empathy.

I believe that religion still has much to offer us if it can do these things. The first is to move away from its conservative ways and nostalgia for a golden past. The second is to offer us realistic ways of coping with the difficult present and help us to realise our potential as humans. Lastly, it helps us to prepare and be ready to enter through the portals of the New World Order into tomorrow's world, emphasising unity and empathy.

However, I have no doubt that religion will still be with us in a hundred years' time, in one form or another but that it will be radically different from what we know and believe today, which is perhaps just as well.

Chapter Eighteen

The International Auxiliary Language

We would find it much easier to communicate with each other if we all spoke and wrote the same language. I believe that we would be able to understand the problems, difficulties and worries we face together worldwide if we used just the one language, rather than the several thousand, which we have in two hundred countries today. In the past, we made a number of attempts to find ways to deal with this particular problem but whether we like it or not, the difficulty is still there.

The most successful attempt was made over two thousand years ago by the Roman Empire. Imperial Rome brought Latin, which was the language they used, to the very edges of their empire. The victorious Romans insisted that the people whom they conquered used the Imperial language. This helped the Romans to communicate more effectively and bond more closely with the people of the subject nations. This not only served the Romans well, but Latin actually outlasted the Empire itself, and is still with us today in certain circles. We find that doctors and botanists still use it in their work settings. If you walk through a botanic garden, you can still see plants, trees and flowers with Latin labels. Up to the middle of the last century, Latin was still the official language of the Catholic Church, which they used to say Mass and sing hymns.

The Arabs behaved in a similar fashion to the Romans several hundred years earlier, when they brought their new religion of Islam halfway around the world, with Arabic as their main language. It is still widely used and revered in many Middle Eastern countries today.

During the Middle Ages, when Spanish, English, Portuguese, French and other European countries were building up their own little empires, they brought their own national languages to the territories where they did their business, conquered and ruled. A number of countries in South America and Africa still use the invaders' language, even after independence. It is interesting to note here that Texas in the US still uses Spanish as a second language.

One of the most interesting cases of language transference is the case of Ireland, which was ruled by the English in the Middle Ages up to the 1920s. The rulers attempted to suppress Gaelic, which was the native Irish language at the time. They managed to drive down the numbers of those speaking Gaelic, with English becoming the principal language of the country. It is a curious fact in Ireland that less than 5% of the population speak Irish regularly, despite the fact that its the first official and national Language of the country.

It is also interesting to note that two of the most important Irish writers of the 20th century, George Bernard Shaw and James Joyce, wrote all of their work in English, but both made an effort to change the way we use it. Bernard Shaw attempted to produce a phonetic alphabet, while James Joyce's last novel, *Finnegans Wake*, was a wild and woolly cornucopia, which tried to move English on to another level, almost musical in tone. Unfortunately, neither of them took their linguistic experiments any great distance, and both are best remembered for their work in English.

The most notable experiment in this field was carried out in the 19th century by a German Jew called Ludwig Zamenhof (1855-1917), who invented a new language, which he called Esperanto. He produced a book about his new language, which he simply called *First Steps*. This was published in 1897 and it aroused considerable interest at the time. The number of those writing and speaking Esperanto grew and developed and for a time, it looked as if it would become the International Auxiliary Language. The League of Nations showed some interest in adopting Esperanto but this died away in the late 1930s, as the European nations geared up for war and the League lost relevance. Esperanto was banned by the Nazis, but it somehow survived into the present century, with over two million people speaking it today worldwide. In 2015, Esperantists held their one hundredth international conference in Lille, France.

Although Esperanto is reasonably easy to learn and it would probably make life a good deal easier for most of us, neither the UN nor the EU have shown much interest in using it, though I imagine that it takes a small army of translators and interpreters to do their business at multilingual forums and conferences. The reason why Esperanto has never taken off in a big way is possibly because it is an invented rather than an organic language, or because of nationalistic politics or prejudices.

In 1951, another new language, Interlingua, put in an appearance. It was sponsored and promoted by the American-based International Auxiliary Language Association. Like a number of the other languages, it has a Latin base but it has not shown its head over the International parapet in a significant way.

In the future, we will have an international referendum to decide whether we want an auxiliary language, and we will be offered a choice between a number of contenders. Here are a number of reasons why we should vote to accept the auxiliary language.

(1) We will still be able to use our native tongue as a first language.

(2) If we have an International Auxiliary Language, we will find it much easier to communicate with others from different countries.

(3) It will be one of the most significant signs of our maturity as a people.

(4) It will make international communications between states and at multilingual conferences, or when we are moving from one country to another, easier.

Chapter Nineteen

Education for Living

As a global community, we will have two main goals in the field of education, during the later years of this century. The first goal will be to raise the educational standards in the underdeveloped and developing countries, to the standards that we find in the developed First World. The second goal will be to raise the educational standards of the developed world, so that they encourage us to develop more of our potential as individuals and communities, socially as well as academically.

I am aware that some people will consider these as wild dreams and absurd fantasies when we look around at the world that we have today. However, we have come a considerable distance in the last hundred years. I believe that if we put our minds to the work that is coming and prepare for the change we will have to make, we will achieve a great deal more than we can possibly imagine.

I think that we should start in the poorest and the most deprived countries, with a number of pilot projects. They should be offered educational help, facilities and equipment. This should be part of a wide and encompassing educational programme, like the Marshall Plan, which was used after the Second World War to help Europe and Japan recover.

We should train and use indigenous teachers to do the work, starting with simple lessons in reading, writing and arithmetic. This will expand and develop depending on the progress we make. We will use digital media and begin to teach the Universal

Auxiliary Language as soon as possible. When the programme of basic lessons has been established, we will move to help and guide. As soon as possible, we will work to bring the three levels together and integrate them.

The whole process will need to be supervised and monitored by the Resource Archive. That facility will advise on the use of video and other digital media, which will play an increasing part in the educational projects. The work on raising educational levels will be closely monitored and evolve over a forty-year period. Ideally, the underdeveloped and developing areas will gradually disappear, as we become more educated and aware. Eventually, we should have a universal but graded system, accepting that different countries have very different traditions and beliefs as well as prejudices, which will need to be factored into the system adapted and eliminated over a period of time.

The Resource Archive will draw up a donors' list of First World countries, which will help with material resources and manpower, under the supervision of the Global Federation.

With regards to the second goal here, we will move away from the main aim and purpose of education today, which is to prepare students for the workplace. Unfortunately, for too many, college is the end and extent of formal education today. In the future, we will see it as a continuing process, which will run through our working life and into our retirement, right into our last years. We will see education as a lifelong pursuit, with something fresh to show us when we come back to it.

Most of us go through three ages in our lives. In the future, most of us will learn to use them properly and to the best advantage. If we can do this, our quality of life will improve. We will find life satisfying and fulfilling, and it will help us to realise our potential.

Our First Age begins when we are born, and it lasts until we leave full-time school. We are taught, in our earliest years, by our parents. Then we go to kindergarten school for three of four years. This is followed by our formal schooling, which can last till we are seventeen or eighteen. In the future, when we leave school, we will spend two years in social service, at home or abroad. Then we will return to college or take up an apprenticeship.

Then we move into the Second Age – our working years. This is the stage where we work to earn a living, get married, raise a family and learn through experience. Facilitators, counsellors and ombudsman will be available to help and advise us through this period, and there will be opportunities to change, work or start new business, or return to college to upgrade.

Between sixty and seventy, we will move into the Third Age. We will be able to take a preparatory course, to prepare us for retirement, with a thorough health check and a Third Age school, which will offer us advice about the options available. There will be training courses and opportunities to offer service at home and abroad if we want or need it. During this period, we will be offered advice and encouraged to write our autobiography and memoirs. In this way, we can pass on our experience in an informal way.

Looking back on my own life, I can see that I had little or no idea of what was coming in my middle or later years. I certainly was not prepared for the Second Age. I left home in my early twenties, travelled round Britain and was lucky to meet a young man of my own age called Peter Gill in Oxford. He showed me the value of questioning and testing everything. He introduced me to the Bahá'í Faith, which allowed me to see the world in a new and exciting way and brought me to where I met my wife, Anne, who has kept me sane and grounded for the past fifty years.

Nevertheless, I had to wait until I reached the Third Age before I begun to understand what life was about. Since then, I have finished over two hundred paintings and completed four books, including this one, which I regard as my legacy. I could not have imagined doing this forty years ago. It is important to realise that we can work on and develop our resources right to near the end.

Chapter Twenty

Global Hunger

Whatever we may think, world hunger is not inevitable as things stand. As a global community we certainly have sufficient resources to feed every single man, women and child living on the planet just now. Basically, it is bad management on a global scale that finds us with this problem today. If we were prepared to share what we have, organise in a structured way, be prepared and ready for emergencies, we would and will be able to deal with this unfortunate business.

While one accepts that famine, starvation and food insecurities are at times brought on by bad weather, disease, failing crops and other natural causes, we find that wars, insufficient preparations and human greed and incompetence are too often responsible for communal hardships, suffering and unnecessary deaths. Every day we hear of new and fresh disasters in the different parts of the world. Very often, these problems result in communities being wiped out, people wasting away and their growth stunted, or people having to sell their children because they cannot afford to feed them.

When we hear what is happening, many of us feel that there is little we can do to change matters. Occasionally, we feel moved to contribute to charities that claim to be helping to mitigate the troubles in one way or another. They distribute food parcels, bring medical help and teach people how to grow food to help themselves. However, when we do this we are simply touching the edge of the problem: running a little to stand still. The problems are really growing steadily worse, as Climate Change steadily increases year by year.

What we really need is a holistic and determined approach if we are to make a real difference and hope to eliminate it eventually. The United Nations, Oxfam, Médecins Sans Frontières and a number of others undoubtedly do a lot of good work, but they have made little serious difference. I do not feel that we will make a serious effort to tackle world hunger until we have been hit by Climate Change and the Migration Crisis, which may act as a loud wake up call. We may even have to wait until after the Last Great War, and a number of other crises on this scale, before we make the necessary change.

The first significant move of a global response will be when the Global Federation appears on the scene, the precursor of the World Government. One of the first things that it will do will be to set up a Resource Archive, which will do serious research to discover what resources are available and how best to use them.

The first practical moves will involve the underdeveloped countries of the Middle and Far East and Africa. The production of synthetic food stuffs and new, multi-purpose grains will help to resolve some of the problems and difficulties in these areas. The International Voluntary and Youth Corps will help when the International Food Programme is launched by the Resource Archive.

We cannot expect to see all the problems and difficulties of the programme resolved in under thirty years. A Marshall-style programme will be inaugurated at an early stage. The cooperation of states and governments will be required, but this should be available when people see the programme working in other countries. There will be a number of 'Bank-run' programmes publicised and a number of World Fairs will show what has been achieved, in displays and demonstrations.

The work will be monitored and its progress widely reported at the end of every year, as we move towards the end of the century. It is an important goal and it is hoped that World Hunger will simply be a memory as we enter the new era. In the next century, people will look back and wonder why we let it drag on for so long.

Chapter Twenty–One

Philosophy

The term 'Philosophy' comes from the Greek, and literally means 'love of wisdom'. However, a more accurate description is 'reflective inquiry', which is what I want to do in the workbook.

We regard the ancient Greeks as the fathers of philosophy. They were broad minded and wide ranging in their approach to the subject, believing that in observation and reason, they could find satisfactory answers to our most difficult questions and problems.

Basically, philosophy teaches us to think in a coherent and structured way about the meaning of life, our knowledge and beliefs and other matters that concern, perplex or worry us.

Today, there are a quite a number of philosophers with interesting things to say about the past, the present or even the future. But we should be aware that no matter how profound or authoritative they seem, that they are simply recorders, setting down what they thought or believed about certain aspects of the world around them. We should be open and prepared to listen to what they have to say, but we should realise that they often questioned or contradicted what other philosophers thought, and we should be prepared to do the same. As an old man said to me about religions, "They can't all be right, but they could all be wrong."

In the East, we find a different set of philosophers like Confucius, Buddha and Lao Tzu, whose writings and teachings still offer help and advice on how best to live our lives and about the meaning of life to the millions who are still prepared to listen. For many thousands of years, political leaders have used philosophic and religious teachings to strengthen and bolster their authority. The most serious trouble in this area came in the last century, when the communists used the ideas of Marx and the Nazis perverted the ideas of Nietzsche and Darwin to try and unite the people of the world on their own terms.

Today, we need clear-sighted and wide-ranging philosophers, who will help us to make sense of the chaotic ideas that we find around us. We need them to help us to join up the dots and give us some idea of what they think is coming our way, in this strange new, miraculous and terrifying world that is shaping up before us today.

We are lucky to have found a group of thinkers, inventors, dreamers and innovators, whom I call the evolutionists. I believe that they are playing an increasingly important role in shaping our future in the next hundred years. The importance of the concept of evolution has grown and developed, as we have come to realise that it is not simply a reactive process, looking back to where we have come from but that it has a proactive role, which we can use to change our world and the way that we live in it.

A number of the evolutionists saw how we could change plant and animal life early on, and the kind of machines like cars, planes and computers we have made and built during the last century. Some have suggested how we can change ourselves and the world around us in much more positive ways than we could possibly have imagined, thought or considered possible. These changes can come through our consciousness or super consciousness, as Colin Wilson suggested, through our attitude towards education and work life (Greta Thunberg), by considering the ways that we build cities or use economics (Jacque Fresco), see religion and science working together

(Bahá'u'lláh), our attitude towards nature and our global home (James Lovelock), our use of computers (Tim Berners-Lee) and the way we look at history and fiction (H.G. Wells).

These are only some of the pioneers who are showing us our way to a better life. Some who will help us to join up the dots, fill in the blanks, show us how to work, love and dream of a brave new world and a beautiful people, with a positive new way of living.

Our human race is entering a fresh and very different phase, where the goalposts have been changed even more than they were in the past hundred years, and we may not even recognise the landmarks or the way that people act. I have no doubt that the philosophers will play their part and help us to find a way, with satisfactory answers to our most difficult questions and problems.

Chapter Twenty–Two

Science and Technology

In today's world, science is mainly concerned with the examination of material reality. It works though the processes of speculation, examination, exploration and tests. If the material survives the tests, it usually comes into practical use, or is used for the basis for further experiment.

The main branches of scientific inquiry include physics, chemistry, biology, astronomy and their numerous subdivisions. Science can be distinguished from technology, which is the application in practice of the findings of science.

Very often, we find that science and technology work so closely together that they are often regarded as the same discipline and regarded as indistinguishable, because they have the same practical end in view. We find that they are both pushing forward, searching for better ways to do things, and they have often achieved results beyond the wildest expectations of our imaginations.

In some quarters, the achievements of science are regarded as among the greatest accomplishments of human intelligence, though it must be admitted that science has been used by politicians and others in truly dreadful ways, which have the potential to extinguish life on the planet but on the whole, science has been a force for great good and a boon to all of us. We have seen technology achieve some remarkable results in different fields, especially in the way that cars, planes and computers have evolved and developed, also how we have been able to use electricity to light up our lives and our cities, and how computers have changed the way that we do business and communicate.

When we look back, we can see how science has made some striking strides in improving our lifestyles, health and well-being, especially in the medical sphere. It has found cures and ways to deal with leprosy, tuberculosis and cancer, and a host of other once-fatal diseases. During the recent pandemic, the World Health Organisation played a vitally important role in guiding and shaping the approach of the majority of nations worldwide, towards how to tackle the virus by changing our behaviour and then, by remarkably coming up with vaccines in a very short time.

In the future, we can expect to see more striking and remarkable developments and successes in these and other fields, sometimes in places that we hardly expect. Looking ahead, technology will help to ensure that we see the smooth running of operations in the New World Order, with the counting of votes for the First World Parliament, allowing us to travel round the world in ninety minutes, rather than ninety days and helping us to grow different and healthier food to feed the poor and the deprived in underdeveloped and developing nations.

Not only that, but I can see science helping us to live well beyond the one hundred and twenty-two-year-old record of long liver, Jeanne Calment, who died in 1997,. We will also explore inside our own heads and possibly insert chips to explore, measure and understand the different aspects of consciousness. We may even be able to move back and forward through time, as easily as we travel to China, New York or the North Pole today.

I am fully aware that much of this may sound extremely fanciful now, but I have no doubt that we will establish permanent bases on the Moon and Mars before the end of the century. If we can concentrate on trying to realise our potential as individuals and a species, we will be able to work more closely together, develop greater empathy and an awareness of how much more we can achieve by learning, rather than taking from others.

I certainly would not be surprised if we find robots, clones and androids performing manual work on the streets, teaching in schools and universities and nursing in hospitals. It is even possible that machines will paint pictures, write books of all kinds and make movies without supervision. They will also perform at the Olympic Games and at the World Song Contest. We may even be able to choose clone partners, monitor old folk homes, and run cities or even countries, in the way that Jacque Fresco suggested. Who knows?

We will find that science and technology will transform our lives, but perhaps the greatest and impressive changes will come when science and religion manage to come to terms with each other. There will be a gradual acceptance that they are compatible rather than competitive disciplines. At present, science is in the ascendant position but in the second half of this century, it is very possible that things will alter radically. If science, religion, art and philosophy were able to work together with some of the other disciplines, goodness knows what we could achieve. The Renaissance and the Islamic Caliphate are examples of when this happened.

It has been suggested that science and religion are like the two wings of a bird, which not only allow it to fly but give it the power and ability to soar into the deep heavens and perform the wildest aerobatics in flocks and murmurations. As I see it, religion can provide us with the visions of a new and more extraordinary world, with the ethics to keep it balanced, while science and technology will help us to achieve our potential and turn our wildest dreams into practical reality.

Section Five

~ The Next Step ~

Chapter Twenty-Three

The Next Step

This workbook is a call for change. I hope that it will start some conversations, suggest discussions, encourage movement and action, and bring about radical change. Looking back, I think that it provides you with more questions than it does radical action and reasonable answers, and this is why I regard it as a workbook.

I would like to think that the book will not only be read but that it will be used to find answers to some of the questions I ask here. Hopefully, it will be used at summer schools and find its way into schools and colleges and universities, television and social media. I do hope it will allow us to look more closely at evolution and the way we teach history.

At present, the teaching of history in schools gives pupils an idea of where they came from, how we developed, and asks what has made us what we are today. However, it has not always had the desired effect and we do not seem to be able to use the information that we receive in productive ways. We need to start teaching about the future, so that we can look at our options.

After the Second World War, the United Nations was set up to keep the belligerent nations apart, but a serious study of history would have realised that this was too timid a move. We should have been striving to achieve a United World instead of a United Nations. If we had been able to work for world peace as hard as we worked to wage world war, who knows what we could have achieved? Possibly much, much more.

In a way, we tried to make things easy for ourselves and attempted to move forward without radical change. We now have an opportunity to do this, rather than wasting another hundred years with pointless bickering, fighting and competing. We could be using the measuring rod of evolution to invent a brave new world for ourselves and our children. We can and will do this if we are prepared to make the changes that are required and are necessary.

This workbook simply points in the direction that we need to take. I would be happy to see others take up the call for change and action, to fill in the dots and work on the big picture.

With regards to the next step, I think that we should do all we can to let people know what is coming and how we should approach it. That is one of the main objectives of this workbook, and I find that we will just use it at summer schools and into the educational system and social media.

I hope to set up a website, where I will be able to report on progress as we move towards Unity. I would love to hear from you with positive suggestions and criticism. Your contribution is important, as each of us has a part to play in this project.

I would like to mention that there is no claim to copyright on this book. I do hope that it gets rewritten and updated every ten years, until we reach the Unity. Is that too much to ask?